The Easy Guide for Finding Your Next Career

Top 10 Lists on Job Preparation, Resumes, Interviews, and Transition

By
Karen Bragg-Matthews

Copyright@2016 by Karen Bragg-Matthews

All rights reserved. No part of this book may be reproduced, stored in a retrieval system, transmitted in any form, by any means, electronic, mechanical, photocopying, recording, or otherwise, without the express written consent of the publisher, except in the case of brief excerpts in critical reviews or articles. All inquiries should be addressed to Karen Bragg-Matthews.

ISBN: 1542682568
ISBN13: 978-1542682565

Cover Designer: Alicia White
Editors: Dolores Bragg and Angela Bragg

Disclaimer: Please note that all company names, addresses, telephone numbers, and websites were accurate at the time of publication and every effort was made to describe the information in this book very accurately as of the publication date. However, companies make periodic changes to their websites, practices, and policies and so this information is subject to change. You should check directly with each company for the most up-to-date information, regarding their practices, policies, pricing, etc.

CONTENTS

How to Use This Book

Section 1 - Preparation

Find Your Dream Job! – Components of a winning job / **1**
Getting Ready to Fly the Coop – Things to keep in mind before you leave your job / **4**
Your Career 411 File / **6**
Interesting Job Search Facts / **7**
Assessments to Take When Looking For a Job / **8**
Places to Look For a Job / **10**
Good Reasons to Quit Your Job / **13**
Danger Signs You Might Be Out of a Job / **15**
Personal Branding / **17**
Network with Confidence / **19**
Revealing On-line Job Search Facts / **22**
LinkedIn Job Search Strategies That Work! / **23**
Make Yourself Visible - Ways to attract people to your profile page / **25**
Boost Your Career Search - Secrets to a successful job hunt / **28**
Company Research Questions / **31**
Stop Wasting Your Time – Job hunting mistakes to avoid / **32**
Job Exit Tips / **35**

Section 2 - Cover Letters and Resumes

Make Sure You Have a Good Cover Story - Cover letters tips / **39**
Types of Cover Letters / **42**
Special Rules for e-Mail Cover Letters / **44**
The Benefits of a Great Resume / **45**
Anatomy of a Resume / **46**
Keyword Tips / **48**
Transferable Skills / **50**
Rules for Resumes / **52**
Resume Don'ts / **54**
Why Use a Chronological Resume / **56**
Advantages of a Functional Resume / **57**
Tips for Uploading Your Resume / **58**
Checklist for Writing Your Government Resumes / **60**

Section 3- The Interview

How to Nail the Information Interview / **64**
Your Interview Tool Kit / **66**
Phone interview Tips / **67**
Video Interviewing / **68**
How Do I Fill This Thing Out: Tips to quickly and professionally complete a job application / **70**
Women – Put Your Best Foot Forward / **72**
Men – Put Your Best Foot Forward / **73**
Interview Attire Don'ts / **74**
Important Things to Do Before the Interview / **75**
Quick Tips to Ace Your Interview / **76**
Ways to Botch an Interview / **78**
Employers Really Want to Know / **80**
Winning interview Strategies / **83**
Mastering the Behavior/Situational Interview / **86**
Signs Your Interview is Going Well / **88**
Signs Your Interview is Not Going Well / **89**
Questions to Ask Yourself After the Interview / **90**
Do You Know What Your References Are Saying About You? / **91**
Thank You Letter Tips / **93**
The Follow-up Phone Call / **95**
Salary Negotiation Tips / **96**
Make a Smooth Transition to Your New Job / **98**

Section 4 - Resources

What Does a Career Coach Do? - Reasons to hire a Career Coach / **103**
Management/Leadership Books / **104**
Finding Work After the Age of 40 Books / **105**
Personal Development Books / **106**
Work/Life Balance Books / **107**
Research Company Websites / **108**
Cover Letter Books / **109**
Resume Books / **110**
10 Books That Will Boost Your Job Search / **111**
Salary Websites: Find Out What You Are Really Worth / **112**

About the Author

Acknowledgements

There are many people I want to thank for their support and assistance in the development and completion of this book.

My husband, Darrick, and children, Edward and Lauren, who have been my constant champions and continue to amaze me with their insight, love and support.

I owe appreciation to my pragmatic and talented sister, Angela Bragg, who could always be counted on to keep me on the straight and narrow.

I want to give a special "shout out" to Alicia White, who is an amazing graphic designer and accountability buddy who has helped throughout this whole process.

I give a very special thank you to my mother and late father, Dolores and Louis Bragg, for the unconditional love, encouragement, and constant source of strength. They have read drafts and contributed countless helpful suggestions.

I am grateful to my friends, family and network, who provided me with unwavering moral support.

My coaching clients who have inspired me with their positive energy and to you, the reader, who have the gumption to pick up this book and read it.

How to Use This Book

You're a busy professional who is thinking about making a job or career change. You know that the way to find new job opportunities has probably changed since the last time you were in the job market or maybe, you just need to refresh the methods and techniques that you already know. Yet, with the hours you devote to your job and other commitments, you really don't have time to sit down and read several "how to" books to get your job search started. *The Easy Guide for Finding Your Next Career – Top Ten Lists on Job Preparation, Resumes, Interviews, and Transition* is your answer. There is a lot of great information in this book to help you take the first steps in your job search if you do not know where to begin. Or, you may only need help with a few aspects of your job search so you don't have to read the whole book. You are able to target and skim the topics that most interest you, design a plan, and take action (this is the most important part). With *The Easy Guide for Finding Your Next Career – Top Ten Lists on Job Preparation, Resumes, Interviews, and Transition,* you are quickly able to pinpoint the information you need and keep the focus on your job search.

The Easy Guide for Finding Your Next Career – Top Ten Lists on Job Preparation, Resumes, Interviews, and Transition has four sections with each section representing a different phase of your job search. Each section contains topics with a list of tips that will assist you with successfully moving your job search along.

Section One - Preparation

Preparation is the key to any successful job search. Most people start by preparing their resume first without having any idea what job they want next. Mental preparation is important and in most cases, more important than preparing a resume and cover letter or doing the research on a prospective company. If you know why you are looking for a new job, your values, and what you stand for, it will better prepare you to embark on your job search. The Preparation section provides you with essential tips to focus on, what you want to do next, and how to get started in the right direction.

Section Two - Resume and Cover Letters
When was the last time you updated your resume? Was it the last time you looked for a job? Resume formats are constantly evolving and vary depending on where and how they are to be submitted. It is better to have an updated resume and not need it than to need it and not have it. This section provides you with tips on how to prepare a resume that tells your best story for the specific position for which you are applying. Even if you are perfectly content with your current job, you still need to up-date your resume to include your accomplishments each year, before you forget.

Section Three – Interview and Follow-up
Everyone knows how to interview, right? Maybe! Today, employers use many different types of methods to interview candidates. Do you know what they are and what to expect? Once again, the right kind preparation is very important to a successful outcome. As a Human Resources Manager, I've interviewed hundreds of people and I can tell you what will work for you and definitely, what doesn't. Many job offers have been lost because the job candidate was not prepared for that specific type of interview. The Interview and Follow-up section contains tips that will help you progress through the various stages of the interview process and gives you advantages over the competition.

Section Four – Resources
The lists in this section contain a number of resources that will help you in your job search and career advancement. Each resource contains more detailed information which will assist you in the various stages of your career.

Why I Use a List Format

Lists
1. Only require the right topic heading for understanding; "deep" thinking is not required
2. Are easy ways to read and retain information
3. Enable you to quickly identify and focus your attention on important points
4. Allow you to scan and select the information you need
5. Are succinct, with information delivered in bite size pieces

6. Reinforce information you may already know
7. Give you a clear outline of everything you need to do to make your job search successful
8. Allow you to organize and execute your job search, mentally checking off each step one-by-one

The Easy Guide for Finding Your Next Career – Top Ten Lists on Job Preparation, Resumes, Interviews, and Transition is a comprehensive resource filled with practical tips and proven strategies. Whether you're beginning your first job or have been in the job market for decades, this book is for you. You will find that the right job search information is at your fingertips.

Let's get started!

PREPARATION

The biggest mistake that you can make is to believe that you are working for somebody else. Job security is gone. The driving force of a career must come from the individual. Remember: jobs are owned by the company, you own your career.

Earl Nightingale

Preparation

1. Find Your Dream Job! – Components of a winning job

2. Getting Ready to Fly the Coop – Things to keep in mind before you leave your job

3. Your Career 411 File

4. Interesting Job Search Facts

5. Assessments to Take When Looking For a Job

6. Places to Look For a Job

7. Good Reasons to Quit Your Job

8. Danger Signs You Might Be Out of a Job

9. Personal Branding

10. Network With Confidence

11. Revealing On-line Job Search Facts

12. LinkedIn Job Search Strategies That Work!

13. Make Yourself Visible - Ways to attract people to your profile page

14. Boost Your Career Search - Secrets to a successful job hunt

15. Company Research Questions

16. Stop Wasting Your Time – Job hunting mistakes to avoid

17. Job Exit Tips

Find Your Dream Job!
Components of a winning job

Everyone's idea of a dream job is different; however, there are several common factors that will help you find the ideal working situation for you. These are some of the main factors to consider.

1. Determine what is truly important to you
To be respected and recognized for your knowledge, help other people, having time for friends and family, or be free of organizational rules and norms, these are just a few examples of work values. Our values are what we care about most and some of our values are more important than others. When our work supports our most important values, each day has a heightened sense of meaning. How well does your job support your values? Take some time to think about what really matters to you.

2. It fits your life style
Finding a job that fits your lifestyle can be challenging. Look for work that allows you to balance effort and achievement with satisfaction, happiness, and a sense of well-being in the most important areas of your life.

3. Money, money, money….money
How much money do you need to earn to be happy? When asked how much, just over half of people surveyed in CNN Money's American Dream poll said it would take less than $100,000. Nearly a quarter of the people who took the poll said between $50,000 and $74,999. This study found that emotional well-being rose with income, but not much beyond $75,000. That means, your compensation package should enable you to have a good quality of life; however, past a certain income, your happiness comes from other factors.

4. You are surrounded by the right people
Do you prefer to work with well educated, creative and like-minded colleagues, or do you like challenging and eclectic cohorts? Describe the characteristics of the people who will bring out the best in you. Very few of us work in isolation and we will need the help of others in order to do our jobs well. You spend the majority of your day at work, so you need to be surrounded by people whom you can respect and build a positive working relationship.

5. How far do you want to go? Location, location, location
Do you prefer a job downtown, uptown, in the suburbs, or at home? Do you want to walk or bike to work; or would you prefer to take public transportation? Do you prefer a short or long commute to work? How much time do you *really* want to spend commuting back and forth to work? The right work location can add valuable time to your day.

6. Hours…One size does not fit all
Do you want to work part time or full time? Would you prefer to start at 8:00 a.m. or 10:00 a.m., or would you like some leeway in deciding your hours of work? Research shows that employees who have control over their work schedules are more motivated and committed, which reduces turnover and burnout. Working hours that fit your life enables you to better balance your life with other responsibilities and manage your schedule according to your needs. With the right hours you can also save time during your commute and reduce the daily rush hour stress.

7. Engage in the type of work you like to do
Although there are many possible reasons for job dissatisfaction, one key factor is the incompatibility of the job with your interests and skills. If you want more job satisfaction, select a job which enables you to use skills, interests, and talents that you want to use.

8. It provides the right amount of challenge
An ideal job should provide an opportunity to learn new things and expand your skill set. It is an opportunity for growth. When you are able to stretch beyond your current comfort level and acquire new skills, that is when growth occurs.

9. Motivation
Motivation is essential to living a productive life. It gives you a sense of purpose and brings your personal vision, values, and life goals into focus. Both challenge and motivation give you an opportunity to prove yourself and consistently perform your best.

10. You are able to envision the future you want
You may not continue to do this specific job or remain in the same place of employment; however, the skills that you have acquired, your experiences and your work connections enable you to envision your next career steps. Your dream job will make you feel that the time you are spending on this job is worthwhile because you are moving toward your ultimate career goals.

Getting Ready to Fly the Coop
Things to keep in mind before you leave your job

Before you pack up your personal belongings and run out the office door to your new found freedom, you should first prepare for your career transition. Here are some things you can start working on today to help you fly the coop.

1. Start or Continue to Build Your Network
Networking is important for gathering information, advice and referrals, but more importantly, it is giving and sharing. Networking is relationship building. Start building good working relationships inside the company and diversify your contacts outside the company. If you are staying in the same industry, try to meet people who work in other parts of your industry and those who have similar functions in other industries. Social networking sites like Facebook, LinkedIn and Twitter are excellent places to connect quickly with a number of people in multiple geographic locations.

2. Check your credit score
Many employers will check your credit score to determine if you pose a security risk and will not hire you if your credit score is too low.

3. Make sure you can pass the pre-employment drug test and/or physical
Your new job may be contingent upon you passing these tests. Employers will usually test you after an offer has been made and before you start your new job. As a Human Resources Manager, I was always surprised with the number of people who failed the drug test and swore it was because there were too many poppy seeds on that sandwich bun they ate the night before!

4. Check your social media accounts
Make sure there is no embarrassing, controversial or unprofessional content that can derail your future plans.

5. Meet with potential references
Ask their permission to use them as your reference and get an idea about what they might say about you. This will give you a chance to fill them in on some of your accomplishments.

6. Investigate your healthcare options
What health care options do you have? You may have an opportunity to continue your healthcare through COBRA benefits, be added to your spouse's healthcare plan, or you may have to purchase healthcare on the open market. Regardless, find out how much it will cost. If you are moving from one employer sponsored insurance plan to another, what is the waiting period before the new plan kicks in.

7. Save before you go.
Make sure you have enough money saved to tide you over until your next pay check from your new employer. If you are starting your own business, get a handle on your expenses. Determine your personal and household monthly expenses and start saving! It is a great relief knowing that you can meet you basic financial needs.

8. Collect materials
Think through the types of material and documentation you might need in the future. These would include performance appraisals and positive correspondence from customers, co-workers, and supervisors. Secure emails and phone numbers of people you want to add to your network or remain in contact. Collect materials you have produced that are not proprietary, this should be part of your "Your Career 411 File – see page 6."

9. Have a Positive Attitude
Use the time you have at your job to build some new skills, experiences, and contacts that will enable you to build bridges out of your current situation.

10. Develop a Plan
You know it is time to leave your job. Develop an exit plan even if you cannot implement it right away. When you know you are taking steps to create a different future for yourself, you can put your current situation in the right perspective and make it more tolerable.

Your Career 411 File

One important thing to do is to keep track of your efforts at work and document your achievements. This can be done by starting and maintaining a Career 411 File. This will be the one place you use to gather data, document your contributions, and track your career progress. It is very easy to do; just place the following information in a regular file folder.

Your Career 411 file should contain:

1. Job description

2. Performance appraisals

3. Positive e-mails from customers and clients

4. Samples of any original work you developed or produced like brochures, programs, etc.

5. A list of projects that were completed on time, before time, and under or on budget

6. Statistics such as your beginning case load, project, client, revenue and sales numbers

7. Positive comments made by your boss and/or peers concerning your work

8. Classes completed and seminars attended

9. Honors, awards, and recognitions

10. Outside groups and organizations to which you belong

Interesting Job Search Facts

1. **80%** of available jobs are never advertised

2. Over **50%** of employees find their jobs through networking (friends, family, co-workers, and acquaintances)

3. **26.7%** of new hires get their jobs through employee referrals (networking and connections)

4. **96%** of job seekers apply to job posted on line

5. **2.3%** of external new hires who walked in the door and applied

6. The average length of a job search is **16.9** weeks

7. **35%** of employers use credit report history as a means of judging personal responsibility

8. The length of an interview is **40** minutes

9. It takes an average of **8** days to hear back from an employer regarding their hiring decision

10. **75%** of employers expect or appreciate a thank-you note after an interview

11. **2.3%** of employees find their jobs through private employment services

Source: LinkedIn, Wall Street Journal, Statistic Brain Research Institute, U.S. Department of Labor, Monster, Indeed, Bureau of Labor Statistics

Assessments You Can Take

Career assessments can help you understand your personality, rediscover talents, and uncover interests that you have taken for granted or long forgotten. The following assessments are just a few of the more widely used and will give you ideas about your next job or career opportunity.

1. Strong Interest Inventory
Learn how your interests, preferences and personal styles can help you discover a fulfilling career. This inventory measures career and leisure interests and has been used for over 80 years.

2. Myers-Briggs Type Indicator (MBTI)
Learn your character type and the character types of other people whom you may know or work with. You will also learn your personality preferences. Based on 50 years of research, the MBTI will help you determine your strengths and possible blind spots. It has a precise multi-dimensional summary of your personality.

3. DISC
This assessment measures your Dominance, Influence, Steadiness, and Conscientiousness. It enables you to better understand your work style and how to build more effective relationships. You learn about the strengths and challenges of your behavior style.

4. Campbell Interest and Skills Inventory
This assessment helps you understand how you fit in the world of work by comparing your results with people who are successfully employed in the fields you are interested in. It also provides an estimate of the confidence in your ability to perform various occupational activities.

5. Jackson Vocational Interest Inventory (JVIS)
JVIS is an education and career planning tool that will give you a snapshot of your interests and how they relate in professional and academic areas. Find it at JVIS.com.

6. Enneagram
It is an assessment that identifies your dominating personality type. Using numbers 1-9, it identifies a range of attitudes and behaviors in the form of unique assets and liabilities.

7. Minnesota Importance Questionnaire (MIQ)
MIQ measures an individual's vocational needs and values. There are six vocational values: achievement, comfort, status, altruism, safety, and autonomy. There are 20 vocational needs identified as a subset of the six values. It is available through **www.psch.umn.edu**. The standard MIQ report gives the information for 90 benchmark occupations grouped into six occupational reference clusters (ORC.) The corresponding index and predictor measures the likelihood of you being satisfied with each of the occupations and ORC.

8. Motivational Appraisal of Personal Potential (MAPP)
It is a career assessment used to find a career that fits with your interests and is linked to a database of career options. It offers information regarding your temperament, vocational interests, aptitude, preferences, and learning style. MAPP is available through Assessment.com.

9. Self- Directed Search (SDS)
SDS is a widely used assessment designed to help you learn about yourself and your career options. There are versions for college students who want to choose a major, veterans entering the civilian job market, or adults pursuing a career change; just to name a few. Your preferred occupation and work environment are categorized into six types: Realistic, Investigative, Artistic, Social, Enterprising, and Conventional. It will help you choose careers and fields of study that best match your self-reported skills and interests. It is available at self-direct-search.com.

10. Keirsey-Temperment Sorter (KTSII)
KTSII is a personality self-assessment that helps you gain insight about yourself and the people around you. It is available at Keirsey.com

Places to Look For a Job

Don't you wish there was one place you could turn to when you are looking for a job? Unfortunately, that one place does not exist; therefore, you must try many different strategies to find a job. Using a combination of job search methods is essential for a successful job search.

1. Networking
Often referred to as the "hidden job market," networking is the best way to find a job. The best positions are not advertised and most highly qualified candidates should put more energy into networking rather than filling out applications on-line. Between 60 and 85 percent of all jobs are secured through networking contacts you have developed or will develop. Networking is for everyone and it does get easier once you commit yourself to doing it.

2. Internet Social Networks
The vast majority of job openings are never posted. They are filled through employee referrals, social media recruiting, and the hiring manager's personal network. That is why it is important that you have a professional profile on internet sites like LinkedIn, Facebook, Twitter, etc., and build a large network of connections. It is best to have as many quality first degree connections in your network as possible. Include individuals from all your previous places of employment, alma mater, volunteer, and charitable organizations. You are able to reach out to your network when looking for a job and employers and recruiters are able to find you.

3. Professional Organizations and Networking Groups
Joining a professional organization can be valuable on many levels. You have an opportunity to get involved and get your name out there. Simply joining an organization will not help in your job search, or get you a job. Getting involved, however, gives you more exposure and access to other professionals which increases your networking circle. Networking groups specifically designed for this purpose may be worth looking into, if for nothing else than to practice your skills. Find these groups through your local Chamber of Commerce, Public Library, or the Internet.

4. Target Companies
Identify the companies you want to work for and proactively market yourself to these companies. Research the company and tell them how you can benefit them. Send the specific hiring manager your cover letter, resume, and reference portfolio.

5. Internet Sites and Postings
Going on-line is now the most common (and frustrating) way to look for a job because it is quick and easy with a variety of sources. There are hundreds of sites to visit when looking for employment including: online job boards, communities, newspapers, and employer websites. It is best to search as many job boards as possible then narrow your search to those that specialize in your particular career field or industry. Register with these sites to receive email. You will learn about relevant vacancies sent directly to your email address. Be aware that your on-line campaign may expose you to potential privacy risks. Always protect your personal information. If you are employed, use extra caution if you don't want your current employer to find out you are looking for another job.

6. Search Firms and Employment Agencies
Only 4% of people find jobs through recruitment agencies. There are several different types of firms and agencies: federal /state, private and those retained by employers. Some agencies list all types of jobs, but most specialize. Register with several agencies. They can be especially useful if you have specialized skills that are in demand.

7. Classified Ads in Newspapers or Trade Journals
Job listings in the classified ad section are minimal because most companies have elected to post their ads on line. Instead of limiting your job search to the classified section, scan the whole paper for employment leads, especially the business section. You can research companies that are placing large ads, or have articles indicating they are doing well and interest you.

8. Cold Call Companies
Applying in-person, in response to "Help Wanted" signs may work if you are applying for hourly or retail jobs. This is one of the least effective ways to find a job in other fields. However, this approach can be a benefit to you because you might be able to acquire useful information. The receptionist can supply you with names of the decision maker and what his schedule is like. The best outcome you can hope for with this approach is to be able to sit down with HR or hiring manager and present yourself. So, make sure you bring your resume and any other pertinent information, just in case.

9. Job/Career Fairs
Many major employers participate in career fairs to meet and hire people. Career fairs can provide general information about career options and specific information about current and future job openings. Usually employers have company literature, brochures, job descriptions and advertising materials. There are many benefits to attending a career fair. You can attend a career fair to look for a job and gather information about the company. A career fair allows you to meet company representatives face to face and develop networking contacts. There are many employers all under one roof and all there to talk with you about career opportunities. This saves you time, money (gas is expensive), and maximizes your job search.

10. College Placement Departments, Alumni, and Military Associations
Having a common bond like attending the same school, or belonging to the same organization is a great starting point when seeking career assistance. Most colleges and universities provide career support for alumni. Colleges and universities usually publish alumni directories which can be an excellent source of networking contacts. If you have targeted a few companies or an industry, you may be able to search the directory to find "fellow alumni" who are working in that targeted company/industry. These contacts can serve as a source for informational interviews and to learn more about open positions in the field you are interested in. Begin your search on-line through social networks such as LinkedIn or Facebook, look for an alumni group in your area, or visit your alumni group's website.

Good Reasons to Quit Your Job

Always look out for your own best interest! If any of these situations exist in your current job, then it is time to change jobs.

1. Your company is in trouble
You see the signs. Your company is losing customers, losing money, and there is no new business coming in. You don't want to be the last one to turn off the lights. Leave before everyone else in your company starts competing for the same positions you are seeking.

2. Your company is ethically bankrupt
Remember Enron and Arthur Anderson? These giant companies died quickly because they were ethically bankrupt. When they shut their doors, thousands of employees were out of a job. What made matters even worse, many of the employees were considered "untouchable" and were not hired by other companies because they were guilty by association. If you know your managers are not telling the truth to customers about the quality of the products, fudging the numbers to make the financial picture of the company look better, or engaging in any other unethical or illegal practices, leave as soon as you can. Do not compromise your ethics.

3. You hate going to work
On Monday, you start looking forward to the weekend and on Sunday afternoon you dread the thought of dragging into work on Monday. Have a clear understanding about why you hate your current position. If you can't change whatever "it" is or your attitude about it, then it is time to consider other options.

4. You are not challenged
A job that does not allow you to grow professionally and expand your skills makes you frustrated, resentful, and bored. If you seek opportunities that just don't exist in your company, then it is time to start fresh with a new job.

5. There is no room for advancement
You have reached a plateau. An environment that offers no room for you to move up, take on more responsibility, receive promotions, or rewards is not a good place for you to remain.

6. Your boss hates your guts
There is some reason that you and your boss don't see eye to eye. A manager has a huge impact on your career. Your boss is the person who makes the decisions about your "plum" assignments, salary increases, or whether you get promoted. If you have made every effort to get along with your boss and things have not changed, then your relationship is beyond repair. Let's face it; your manager is not going anywhere, so it is time for you to move on.

7. You get physically ill
Migraines, insomnia, depression, anxiety, and other ailments are signs that you are probably under a great deal of stress from your job. Life is too short to be miserable. When your job is taking a toll on your physical and mental health, then it is definitely time to change jobs.

8. Your life situation has changed
You have reassessed your work/life situation and decided that what you are doing no longer works for you.

9. You have burned your bridges
You lost a major account, disclosed confidential information, or maybe you are known as a major kiss-up. Your reputation has been destroyed. In most cases, it will take a very long time to rebuild your reputation. It will probably be to your advantage to cut your losses and find a new job.

10. You have not received a raise in several years
Many companies froze or reduced employee pay during the economic downturn; however, the economy is now turning around. You should not have to continue to suffer just because your company is still recovering. There are many job opportunities outside of your company. Stop making excuses, get your resume in order, brush up on your interview skills, and get out there!

Danger Signs You Might Be Out of a Job

Just because you are paranoid doesn't mean they are not out to get you! Being fired can come without warning. However, usually there are numerous signals that your days of employment are numbered. It is a good idea to be aware of some of these key danger signals beforehand so you will be prepared.

1. You messed up "Big Time"
Were you responsible for losing a major customer or account? Was your expense report heavily padded, or did you come to work smelling like whiskey, and wearing the same clothes as the day before? You might get a reprimand, if your company is more benevolent; however, if they are in a tough financial situation and/or in the midst of laying-off staff, count on your name being on the list.

2. Your company recently has been sold or merged
Changing owners means new management and they always have new plans for the company. This usually means that the new owners are looking to cut costs and to eliminate any duplication or redundancy. Unfortunately for you, the new plan will usually include cutbacks and layoffs.

3. Communication levels have changed
There were always tons of emails waiting for your comments or advice; your phone rang non-stop with calls from customers, colleagues, and vendors; and there was always a barrage of text messages. Now communication is down to a trickle.

4. You are set up to fail
You are given a bad territory or have been given an impossible task with a short deadline and no assistance.

5. You are put out of the loop
You are no longer copied on memos or given circulated reports. You are no longer invited to meetings that you regularly attended; or worse still, everyone in the department is invited to attend an important meeting except you! If you were in the know about all things going on in your company, but now you find out the news from everyone else; watch out! This is a tell-tale sign that you are on someone's list.

6. You are disliked by just about everyone especially your boss
If you are in constant conflict with your co-workers and your boss has made comments about your unpleasant personality or attitude, then your days are numbered. If you have a tense or are in a negative relationship with your boss, it does not bode well for your future at the company. If your boss is more critical of your work, begins to monitor or micromanage your work, then this is definitely reason for concern.

7. You are treated like a leper
People stop dropping by to talk and cannot look you in the eye as you walk down the hall; look out! The boss who usually invites you to stop by to give a quick status update hasn't said a word to you in three weeks. When you enter a room, people stop talking and/or abruptly change the subject.

8. Your boss is leaving a paper trail
You receive memos from the boss criticizing your work and pointing out errors. All meetings and discussions with you are documented.

9. You are given a bad performance review
Over the past year, you have done your work and completed all your projects on time. Generally your performance review is a good reflection of your efforts, your accomplishments, and outlined suggested areas of development. However, this time you receive a marginal review and you have been given a performance improvement plan. Many companies compile a list of employees who are considered the lower performers; it looks like you might be part of this list.

10. You have been moved to a position of less responsibility
Your daily responsibilities are being divided among your coworkers or you have been stripped of your responsibilities, and you realize you are doing things with little value to the department. Now you report to someone with much less clout or status than your last boss. Perhaps your new boss is known as the terminator and specializes in the dirty work of cleaning up departments. Your prize subordinate is reassigned and an overqualified new hire or temporary worker appears in the department waiting for the "right job" to open up.

Personal Branding

Personal branding is a method to proactively expand, shape, and control your reputation to position yourself for success. Here's how you can do it:

1. Define Your Niche
You have a unique combination of work and life experiences, and personal characteristics that will help create your niche. Choose an area of expertise or market segment that you know well and understand better than most people in your field. For instance, everyone in your department has a business degree (MBA) and they are detailed oriented, ethical and dependable, but you also go the extra mile for clients, genuinely care about people and you are an excellent relationship builder. Then your brand message should include that you are a business leader who is client focused and an expert in relationship building. Study your competition, deliver something that it does not and own it!

2. Be Authentic
Here's the great part about personal branding; you get to decide what your personal brand is by defining your unique promise of value and with whom you want to share it. Personal branding is about expressing yourself in authentic terms and allowing you to be the person you were meant to be.

3. Be Confident
You develop confidence as you develop your personal brand because you are highlighting your strengths. When you know you have something of value to offer, your confidence soars.

4. Build Strong Positive Relationships
Connect and nurture strong co-operative relationships with friends, coworkers, bosses, and social media community. Show genuine interest in their endeavors, find the common ground and treat everyone with respect and common courtesy.

5. Be Consistent on Social Media
Your image online is just as important as your in-person presence and communication. Whether on LinkedIn, Twitter, Facebook, Google, Instagram or email, you want to make sure your social media sites represent you and your brand well. You want to be clear and consistent

about your message. Every time you communicate with your target audience (customers, co-workers, bosses, and potential employers) your message needs to be perceived the same way.

6. Share Useful Information
Social media allows you to share your expertise with people, with whom you would not normally have regular contact. To build your presence online, you want to share useful information with your target audience, behave professionally, and treat others well. Send information to your connections, at regular intervals, which is consistent with your brand.

7. Develop a Personal Career Brand Strategy
What is the reputation you want to build for yourself? How does your target audience want to work with you or do business with you? What are your specific goals? Pick a date for initiating and completing each of your goals. Set deadlines for yourself and stick to them.

8. Your Image Should Match Your Personal Brand
Realize that you are always on display so your appearance really does matter. Everything you wear conveys information about you. Select clothing that represents who you are and what you stand for. Your goal is to select clothing that will visually help you express your authentic self.

9. How Do Others See You?
To determine the effectiveness of the brand you are creating for yourself, evaluate how others see you. After all, your personal brand exists in other people's perceptions of you. To help determine if your personal brand is in line with the image you are trying to project, ask co-workers and friends to sum up your professional image in a sentence or two.

10. Stay Relevant
Creating your brand is not a one-time event; it is an on-going process. People with strong personal brands continue to evolve by incorporating new knowledge and expanding their goals. To keep your brand relevant, you need to set new goals and accomplish them.

Network with Confidence

Do you breakout in a cold sweat knowing you have to network at the next conference or convention? You are not alone! Networking is an essential skill that enables us to consistently widen our circle of acquaintances and contacts. This helps you broaden your knowledge, increase your visibility and sphere of influence, and can help you make a quick transition to your next job. Here are some tips to help you prepare for your next networking event:

1. Identify what you want to accomplish and who you might want to talk to
Why are you attending this event? Are you more interested in learning, or volunteering for the organization's cause, or are you interested in the type of people who are attending this event? For example: Attending your profession's annual convention is an opportunity to meet fellow members in your profession and learn from "thought leaders," while some events are designed for you to meet as many people and exchange information as you desire.

For introverts, networking can be a very draining experience. Make networking less taxing by concentrating on quality and not necessarily, quantity. If possible look at the profiles of the individuals you wish to connect with to learn about their work and experience. Think through what you want from your interaction with these individuals. At a minimum, you want to make contacts, exchange business cards, email addresses and/or phone numbers.

2. Think about how you want to introduce yourself
We all dread the "what do you do" question because you either don't know what to say or what you say can sound boring. You know the question is going to be asked so get prepared. You want to say something about yourself that is short, concise, and interesting. Which of the following two introductions do you find more interesting and will probably prompt additional conversation?
Example 1: "My name is Karen Bragg-Matthews. My company is KBM Career Concepts and I am a Career Coach."
Example 2: "I help adults figure out what they want to be when they grow up! I am a speaker, writer, and career coach. My name is Karen Bragg-Matthews and I'm CEO of KBM Career Concepts."

Then practice the delivery of your introduction so it sounds natural and smooth.

3. Walk in with confidence and a smile
Upon arriving at the networking event, put a smile on your face, take a moment to look around the room and observe. There will be people standing alone, hovering around the refreshments, or gathered in groups. Depending on your comfort level, it may be easier for you to start a conversation with someone who is standing alone rather than immediately trying to break into a group discussion. Just make sure you continue to make your way around to meet other people.

4. Think about what you can say to initiate conversations that will build rapport.
It might be difficult or intimidating to walk into a room of strangers; however, if you have prepared something to break the ice, it will be much easier. You might ask: "Is this the first time you've attended this event?" or "What do you know about the organization or keynote speaker?"

5. Make sure you have business cards and pen.
The goal is to have meaningful conversations with individuals; not to pass out as many business cards as possible in record breaking time. You want to record notes about your conversations, for example: what you had in common, what you talked about, a follow-up call or meeting time/date.

6. It's not about you…..really
Be interested instead of interesting. People like to talk about themselves. You will be viewed more favorably when you encourage the person to do more talking during your conversation. Show interest in the person you are talking to by asking open ended questions instead of closed ended questions that just require a "yes" or "no" answer. This allows the person to do most of the talking.

7. Listen and be present
Listen and pay attention to what the person is saying. Refrain from thinking of your next question, your response to what they are saying, or scanning the room to see who else you might talk to.

8. Follow-up

Depending on your initial conversation, this may mean a phone call, sending information, setting up a meeting, or connecting on LinkedIn, Facebook and/or Twitter. Make it a rule to follow-up within 48 hours of your initial meeting and be prepared to remind the person who you are and when you met.

9. Be your authentic self

You may dread the thought of networking because you believe you have to prove how good you are; wishing you were someone better. Stop thinking you have to put on an act! Being your authentic self is communicating your skills, talents, and knowledge. It is all the things that are uniquely you.

10. Tell people exactly what you want

Be specific about what you want and be able to explain it clearly. Do you want to meet a certain person at a specific company or level? People are more likely to assist you if they know exactly how they can help you. It is better to find one or two people whom you can connect with in the future rather than to collect two dozen cards that lead nowhere. Offer to help others. When you offer your help, people will want to reciprocate. People are more willing to share information when they feel they are in a mutually beneficial relationship.

Revealing On-line Job Search Facts

1. **245** - Average number of people who apply to a single on-line posting

2. **7%** - Average percentage of online applicants who get interviewed for a single position

3. **1%** - Percentage of job seekers who are successful sending their resume blindly to every job that pops up

4. **9%** - Percentage of job seekers who are successful sending resumes only to targeted companies

5. **90%** - Percent of recruiting firms that do a Google search on candidates

6. **79%** - Percentage of employers who conduct an online search of applicants

7. **35%** - Percentage of hiring managers who immediately screened out candidates based on what was found on their social networking profiles

8. **89%** - Percent of employers who have reported hiring someone from LinkedIn

9. **94%** - Percent of recruiters who are active on LinkedIn

10. **36%** - Percent of job seekers who are active on LinkedIn

Source: LinkedIn, Wall Street Journal, Statistic Brain Research Institute, U.S. Department of Labor, Monster, Indeed, Bureau of Labor Statistics

LinkedIn Job Search Strategies That Work!

Use the number one professional networking site, LinkedIn, to help you find a job. These tips will help boost your career search:

1. **Complete all sections of your profile** – People want to know you and how well rounded you are. In addition to completing the "Summary, Experience, and Education" sections on your profile, make sure you complete the "Additional Information" section which includes your websites, twitter, relevant interests, groups and associations, and honors and awards.

2. **Add relevant search keywords and industry buzz words to your "Summary" and "Basic Information" sections** – Make it easy for prospective employers to find you during their search by including industry buzz words, keywords, and skill sets in your profile.

3. **Connect with your connections** – Who are my connections and who do my connections know? Let your immediate network know about your goals so they can recommend the right people for you to contact.

4. **Strive for quality <u>and</u> quantity** – Measure the success of your network by the depth of the relationships built, leads generated, joint ventures and strategic partnerships, qualified employers successfully contacted and interviews scheduled, speaking opportunities, and publicity opportunities.

5. **Job boards** – The most direct way to find a new job is to search for openings on the LinkedIn job board. You can see what skills are attractive to companies which you can keep in mind as you edit and refine your profile.

6. **Same job different place** – If you are looking for a specific job, one way to approach your job search is to identify people with the same or similar job title or responsibilities. You can find these people by performing an advanced job search for people with similar titles as the ones you are interested in.

7. **Rely on Alumni** – Having a common bond like attending the same school, or belonging to the same organization is a great starting point when seeking career assistance. Search alumni association groups for any school, club, or organization you attended; you can find them in the "Group Directory" or find former classmates by accessing the "Classmates" tab.

8. **Be company focused** – Suppose you know you want to work at a specific company. You can review the LinkedIn profiles of the hiring managers and discover which contacts can introduce you. You can also follow a company through their "Company" page. Spend some time each week reviewing news, job openings, and useful contacts.

9. **Be the "Go To" person** - Join a group and share answers, make comments and demonstrate your expertise to distinguish yourself. Groups provide you access to connect with and contact fellow group members who could become your future co-workers and employers.

10. **Contact the decision maker** – LinkedIn can help you find the person who can make the hiring decision. By performing an advanced search you can identify the head of the department, Vice Presidents, and Directors working for your targeted company. Find the closest person (in your network) to that decision maker and ask your contact for help, a connection, or information to help you reach the next level.

Make Yourself Visible
Ways to Attract People to Your LinkedIn Profile Page

Most career professionals have a LinkedIn profile page, but don't spend the time to write a compelling profile. So how do you stand out from the other hundreds of million members? Here are some things you can to do.

1. Look the part
Stop posing with your dog or cat, unless you are a veterinarian. This is a website for professionals, so you need to have a professional headshot. Your picture needs to be high quality, with good lighting and in sharp focus. Your photo should be recent and you should be forward facing, or looking forward and toward your content.

2. Use the right keywords
Recruiters use keywords to search LinkedIn profiles so make it easy for prospective employers to find you during their search by including industry buzz words, key words, and skill sets in your profile. You can do this by making a list of the terms associated with your skills, experience, and the type of position you are seeking. Find keywords by looking at several job postings to determine what words frequently occur. Insert these words in your headline and throughout your page.

3. Have a compelling headline
The headline is not about you; it is about how you can help the other person. Your headline needs to speak to your target audience and compel them to click on your profile. Don't miss the opportunity to grab the right attention by including key words, how you can assist a company, what you do, or your experience. For example, if you are a business consultant, your headline can read "Helping companies overcome obstacles, create order out of chaos, and improve results." As a marketing professional, your compelling headline can read, "I help you get massive ROI from strategic Marketing, PR and Social Media." You have 120 characters available right below your name and before your location, so use them.

4. Go Hollywood!
You can add videos and images in your summary and experience fields. Use your smartphone to record a portion of your presentation or you explaining some aspect of your job. You will have more visibility, increase your credibility, and definitely look more tech savvy. Make sure to include any pictures of awards or commendations you received.

5. Grow a quality network
Your network is important for gathering information, advice and referrals, but more importantly, it is for giving and sharing. Everyone sees the person who has 500+ connections listed on their profiles. Unfortunately, some individuals race to collect as many connections as quickly as possible, and would not know the majority of the individuals listed if they walked right past them. It is best to have as many quality first degree connections in your network. Include individuals from all your previous places of employment, alma mater, volunteer, and charitable organizations.

Measure the success of your network by the depth of the relationships built, leads generated, joint ventures, strategic partnerships, qualified employers successfully contacted, interviews scheduled, speaking opportunities, and publicity opportunities. These can only come when you know the people in your network, and can make or ask for referrals with confidence.

6. Add recommendations
It is easy and convenient for people to click on your "Skills" to endorse you. It means more when you are able to get a written recommendation. Think about it! Someone has taken their time to recognize you. Recommendations are the only outside verification of your skills and abilities, and employers can see exactly what other people think about you and your work. How do you get recommendations? You ask for them. When someone praises or congratulates you for something you have done, ask them to write what they have just said on LinkedIn. And don't forget to write recommendations for others. Nothing goes further in solidifying a relationship than a sincerely written recommendation.

7. Have a killer summary
Try to use the 2000 characters you are given to tell your unique story about your accomplishments, experiences, or achievements. Spend time developing this section. Your summary is just as important as your picture and headline.

8. Volunteer work
Volunteer work can give you an edge with hiring managers. Just because volunteer work is unpaid does not mean that the skills you learn are of little or no value. Many volunteering opportunities provide extensive training. Volunteering gives you the opportunity to practice important skills used in the workplace; such as, teamwork, communication, problem solving, project planning, task management, and organization. These skills can easily transfer to a new job.

Through volunteer work, you can gain experience and get additional exposure in a new career field. If you wish to change careers, volunteering in that new field demonstrates your commitment to a perspective employer.

9. Highlight courses and certifications
If you are a recent college graduate, add specific courses. This will enable you to list any classes that qualify you for positions you are seeking. Adding certifications to your current career will demonstrate your commitment to your profession.

10. List your hobbies and interests
You never know what might pique the interests or what you might have in common with a hiring manager or recruiter.

Boost Your Career Search
Secrets to a Successful Job Hunt

The people who appear to "get all the breaks" are the ones that have really just done the work to prepare themselves for opportunity. They've put into place the resources, people, and infrastructure to capitalize on an opportunity when it arrives. Here are some steps you can take to help you increase your job search effectiveness.

1. Make a schedule
Commit to a block of time every day to work on your job search. The amount of time you allot depends on your available time. Even if it is only an hour each day, make it count. You don't have to be tied to the computer. Make sure you build in activities that allow you to network and build your network. Vary the way you spend your time so you do not get burned out on one job search activity, particularly if you do not like doing it.

2. Develop a System
You'll need a way to monitor which companies and positions you've applied to and the status of the applications. Tracking is especially important for following up if you've applied and heard nothing from an employer or interviewed with an employer. You'll need to track that information so you can make follow-up phone calls or send an email. Many systems are possible; find one that works for you.

3. List the organizations
Where do you want to work? Start a list of 20-25 organizations that you consider ideal to work for. Your job search is more effective when you have specific organizations to target. Companies will be removed and added to your list. Keep your eyes open for industry competitors and watch for small companies on the move.

4. Research, and follow organizations you want to target in your job search
As you begin to learn more about these companies you will begin to understand what they need and whether you are a fit with their company culture. Refer to –"Company Research Questions"

5. Get insider information
Consider conducting informational interviews. Meet with people who work at your target companies to learn about their business needs. Some of the best research comes from these conversations. Use the information you gather to tailor your resume, cover letter, and interview responses.

6. Have more than one inside contact
Often a job seeker stops acquiring names and meeting with people once they already have an inside connection. Don't stop there. You need to play the odds and have more than one ally. You never know the influence or alliances people have.

7. Track referrals
Of course, networking will be a major part of your job search. You will need to keep track of who referred you and where. You also want to send them a thank you note for the introduction and a status update after you and the referral have met. So few people actually do this, it is an excellent way to say thank you. It demonstrates your professionalism, solidifies your strengths in follow through, and makes you memorable.

8. Reach out every week
It takes longer than you think to set up a meeting with someone. You won't usually be able to schedule a meeting the same week. It is important that you build a pipeline of meetings for each week. This can only happen if you set time aside each week to reach out to people whom you want to meet. Use the referral names you acquired and your list of target companies to create your weekly plan for proactively contacting people you should know.

9. Follow up and follow through
Set reminders for 1 week and every 30 days. You may need to modify these time frames based on the feedback you get. Continue to follow-up until there is closure.

10. Include the right balance of leads
Use job boards, agencies, third party recruiters, career fairs, and alumni associations to round out your job search efforts. However,

the majority of your time should be used to network with people who can connect you to your target companies.

11. Discipline
You need to hold yourself accountable for continuing to stick with your plan. Having discipline means that you can find a way to manage the distractions and roadblocks and still follow through on other things you've committed to.

Company Research Questions

Employers consider company research a reflection of your interest, enthusiasm, intelligence, and commitment. In a very competitive job market, research is your secret weapon to make yourself different by specifically identifying the added value you bring. The following questions will help you learn about the company and help you formulate questions that will help you stand out from the crowd.

1. What does the company do?

2. What are the company's current priorities?

3. What products or services does the company provide?

4. What are its areas of expertise?

5. Who are the company's competitors?

6. What are its greatest accomplishments? What setbacks has it experienced?

7. What are the company's current projects? Is it initiating any new products or projects?

8. What is the company's business philosophy? What is its mission?

9. What is its reputation?

10. What are the company's sales, earnings, and assets?

Stop Wasting Your Time
Job Hunting Mistakes to Avoid

It is easy to get confused and frustrated when looking for a job because it is much more complicated than it used to be. Here are some common mistakes people make when looking for a job.

1. You have no on-line presence
A recruiter will usually research a candidate to find out more about him before being considered for an interview. If you have no on-line presence, that signals to the recruiter that you have had very little to contribute professionally, you are not comfortable with technology, or you have something to hide. Make sure your social media profiles reflect the right image.

2. You do not tailor your resume for each position
Your resume should show that you are a qualified candidate for that specific position; so you need to tailor each resume for each position for which you apply. The recruiter will not take time to determine if you have the required skills to do the job. You must change your key words to match those used in the job posting and emphasize different skills, abilities, and attributes to model the language used in that particular industry. You may also want to highlight different accomplishments, which are more in line with the position you are pursuing.

3. Using the shotgun approach
This means sending out one hundred resumes and hoping one or two of your resumes will get someone's attention. Recruiters are bombarded with hundreds of unsolicited resumes each week and can easily identify a generic resume and cover letter. More than likely, that generic resume will end up in the pile of rejects. Have a plan. Research a specific industry or company; then determine if any of your contacts have a connection which will enable you to get your foot in the door.

4. Relying only on the internet to find a job
It is important to check the various websites for job postings; however, this should not be your only source for looking for employment. You must develop a multifaceted approach to finding

a job. This means combining your internet search with: connecting with your network, doing a targeted job search, and connecting with professional organizations.

5. Not knowing what you want to do
Telling your friends, family, and acquaintances that you will take any type of job does not work. Narrow down the type of positions you are looking for and explain the specific skills you possess with possible job titles. This will enable your contacts to easily keep you in mind.

6. Not dedicating enough time to look for a job
Finding a job is a job. We all know those people who are contacted by recruiters, or have friends and acquaintances who recommend them for positions. It seems as though job opportunities just fall in their laps! The truth be told, it usually happens only after laying a lot of ground work. They usually have built a good professional reputation and solid network.

Finding the time to look for a job is considered a low priority especially if you are currently working. If you are serious about seeking a new career opportunity it is going to take discipline, rearranging your schedule, and/or possibly giving up something you routinely do in order to devote time to your job search.

7. Working on only one job lead at a time
Do not stop your job search when the first employer wants to schedule a phone interview. That phone interview is usually the beginning of a process that can take weeks or months. You do not want to rely on one opportunity coming through; continue to look, network, respond to other leads and job postings, until you have a firm job offer.

8. Keeping your job search a secret
It may be embarrassing to be unemployed; but get over it! The majority of jobs are filled through referrals. Let your network know you are looking for employment.

9. Only pursuing jobs that fit a specific title
A teacher can become a corporate trainer. An outstanding salesperson can sell many types of products. Just because you started

in one industry does not mean you have to remain there your whole working life. Take inventory of your core skills and abilities to determine how they may transfer to a new company or industry.

10. Having a negative attitude
No one wants to help you find a job if you are angry, complaining, or depressed! Employers can certainly spot a candidate who acts like a "know it all" or feels that he is "owed a position." Do your best to be positive and enthusiastic.

Job Exit Tips

You have decided to leave the company. Make sure your exit leaves a positive impression by following these tips.

1. Write a resignation letter and give a two weeks' notice if you are voluntarily resigning. However, if you know you will be escorted out immediately, you will want to time your exit to your advantage.

2. Let your immediate supervisor know you are resigning first.

3. Most companies conduct an exit interview as a courtesy. Attend if you feel comfortable with the process.

4. Watch what you say and be aware that the exit interview can be used against you; avoid the "you have nothing to lose attitude."

5. Be as fair and objective as possible during the exit interview. Be constructive in your evaluation of the job, company and management. You do not want to burn any bridges.

6. If possible, write down what you are going to say in the exit interview.

7. Read all paperwork given to you. There will usually be several forms you will sign. Ask to review them if there is something questionable. Organizations can usually wait a few days.

8. Maintain your composure. Avoid angry outbursts or violent actions.

9. Return any company property like keys, computers, or badges. Make sure you do not take anything that does not belong to you.

10. Continue to do your work and what is asked of you.

COVER LETTERS & RESUMES

Responding to "Help Wanted" ads is very similar to buying a lottery ticket. There eventually will be a winner...but the probability is that it will not be you.

Pam Lassiter

No one creates a perfect resume on their first try. Writing a perfect resume is a messy process, but the easiest way to start is by simply getting in the right mindset and putting pen to paper.

Matthew T. Cross

Cover Letters and Resumes

1. Make Sure You Have a Good Cover Story - Cover letters tips
2. Types of Cover Letters
3. Special Rules for E-Mail Cover Letters
4. Benefits of a Great Resume
5. Anatomy of a Resume
6. Keyword Tips
7. Transferable Skills
8. Rules for Resumes
9. Resume Don'ts
10. Why Use a Chronological Resume
11. Advantages of a Functional Resume
12. Tips for Uploading Your Resume
13. Checklist for Writing Your Government Resumes

Make Sure You Have a Good Cover Story
Cover letter tips

A cover letter tells the reader why you are contacting them and gives you an opportunity to explain how you can contribute to the organization.

1. Always send a cover letter
I know, writing a cover letter is a pain in the behind! However, every resume sent should have a cover letter whether it is mailed, e-mailed or in response to a job posting on line. The person receiving and reading your resume will not have to guess where or how your skills and qualifications will fit with the company's open position.

2. The first impression matters
Before a recruiter reads one word of your cover letter, the weight and the color of your stationery speak volumes about your professional brand. Select high quality paper that is between 18lbs. and 25lbs. Your cover letter stationery should coordinate with the paper used for your resume. Choose a traditional stationery color of white, cream, ivory or very (I mean, very) light gray. Keep in mind, that your cover letter and resume may be copied or scanned. Darker or brightly colored paper will come out dark and your information will not copy or scan clearly.

3. Make it easy to read
Choose a font type that is easy to read. Recommended font types include: Times Roman, Courier New, Garamond, Georgia, Bell MT, Goudy Old Style, Cambria, Arial, Tahoma, Veranda, and Century Gothic. Font point size should be between 10 – 12 pts. Each font type has slightly different spacing so make sure the font point size is also easy to read.

4. Write to someone specific
Cover letters addressed to "To Whom It May Concern" are a turn-off, ignored and quickly filed away. Whenever possible, try to find out who may be making the hiring decisions. You can do this by exploring several avenues; such as, inquiring through your network, researching the internet, through LinkedIn, or contacting the company to get the name of the hiring manager.

5. Your cover letter must be specifically tailored for each job opportunity

Remember, your cover letter should pique the interest and motivate your reader to look at your resume and contact you for an interview. Show them that you know something about the company, who they are and what they do by including information you obtained in your research. If you are applying for an advertised position, use the requirements listed in the advertisement. Include industry terms and phrases that are meaningful to the employer. You can also tailor your cover letter by quoting a relevant article, a recent industry statistic, or an interesting fact about yourself.

6. Limit your cover letter to one page

Keep it simple! Create each cover letter by using the same basic business letter format with your return address at the top, the hiring manager's name, company inside address, a salutation, three to four paragraphs in the body of the letter, closing with your name signed and printed.

7. Watch your tone

Your cover letter is the perfect opportunity to let the "real you" shine through. The content of your cover letter must remain professional; however, this is your opportunity to tailor what you want the hiring manager to know about you. If you are applying for an upper management position, you may want to present your information in a more assertive and straight forward manner. A counseling position may require a softer, yet straight forward tone. Have someone read your letter to make sure you come across the way you intended.

8. Follow a basic three or four paragraph structure

In the first paragraph introduce yourself; explain who you are and why you are applying. The second and third paragraphs should tell a story including what you know about the company and why you are uniquely qualified to fill the position. These two paragraphs should share information that is relevant to your reader's needs. The second paragraph will briefly describe your most important professional skills, significant contributions and academic qualifications. The third paragraph should explain how you can be an asset to the company and include the company research you've done. In the last paragraph, ask for an interview, explain what your next steps are to secure an interview or request that they contact you.

9. Make absolutely no errors
Make sure the person's name and title are correct. Your spelling and grammar must be perfect. Proofread your letter several times or better yet, have someone with good proofreading skills look over your letter before you send it out.

10. Send and follow up
Very few people actually take the initiative to follow up. This will set you apart from other job applicants, add to your credibility and help the reader remember you. It will also help you learn where you stand in your job search.

Types of Cover Letters

There are many types of cover letters; each is used for a specific purpose. In each case, it is important that you tailor your experience, skills and other qualifications.

1. Responding to an advertisement – read the job posting carefully when responding to this type of ad because it will have keywords scattered throughout. Use these keywords in your cover letter to describe your specific skill set as it relates to the job.

2. Blind advertisement – a blind advertisement does not identify the hiring company. Because you may not be able to identify and research the company, it will make it difficult to tailor your letter to the company. Use the job title and reference number in the subject line or look for clues in the ad or email address for your greeting.

3. Cold call letter to an employer – it is an inquiry about possible job openings at a company and it lets the employer know what you are interested in. Your first paragraph must grab the reader's attention in a professional manner.

4. Cold call to a headhunter – the headhunter may work for a local employment agency, on contingency, or be retained by a company. Immediately get to the point by identifying the specific type of job you are looking for, detail your skills, salary requirements and the desired geographic location. Like the cold call letter to an employer, your first paragraph must grab the reader's attention in a professional manner.

5. Letters following a referral – it is important that the name of a person who is referring you to the job or company is mentioned in the first paragraph.

6. Follow-up letter - usually follows a conversation or meeting when the person requests that you send them your resume. Include information that refers back to your meeting to jog the memory of the person concerning your conversation and any specific points you want to reinforce about your unique qualifications.

7. Sponsor letter - you are asking an individual to use their authority to assist you in securing an interview.

8. Direct mail letter – this is also known as a broadcast cover letter. You want to select companies that need your expertise. Tailor your correspondence to capture their attention. This type of letter is most successful for careers that are highly specialized.

9. Broadcast letter –the purpose of this type of letter is to initiate a conversation so it must identify a real or potential need in the company. Your cover letter quantifies your skills and background to meet that need. The format of the broadcast letter can combine the cover letter and resume into one document, or it can be similar to a direct mail cover letter. This letter will usually target a specific type of job or job posting.

10. Networking or referral letter – this letter requests job search advice and assistance. It can be written by another individual who can recommend you for a position; this letter can function as a letter of introduction.

Special Rules for E-mail Cover Letters

1. E-mail cover letter should be part of the e-mail and not an attachment.

2. Construct a subject line that is attention grabbing. Include the desired position and wording that is succinct.

3. You still want to address your email to a specific person. If you do not know that person's email address, browse the company website or call the company to get it.

4. Write a condensed version of your cover letter. Remember, your cover letter, contact information and resume are all contained in this document, so you don't want to overwhelm the reader with a lengthy cover letter.

5. Make sure to include all your contact information. This includes your name, address, telephone number, as well as, your email address in the body of your email.

6. Your email cover letter should include the same information in the first paragraph as a written cover letter. The first paragraph explains who you are and why you are applying.

7. Merge the second and third paragraphs to describe your most important professional skills, significant contributions, academic qualifications, why you can be an asset to the company, and your company research.

8. In the last paragraph, ask for an interview, explain what your next steps are and/or request that they contact you. Mention that your resume is included below in the same document and as an attachment.

9. Include keywords in your cover letter. This will increase your chances of the tracking system identifying you as having the desired skill set and improve the prospect of being selected.

10. Before you press the send button proofread, proofread, proofread. This is the employer's first impression of you; make sure it is positive.

The Benefits of a Great Resume

1. It is a marketing tool that can open the door to an interview.

2. It gives the employer information about you, which is not asked on a job application.

3. It shows off your skills, abilities, accomplishments, and potential.

4. Enables the interviewer to link your talents, skills and abilities to the employer's needs and it will remind the interviewer of your skills and abilities long after the interview is over.

5. It lets you smooth over weaknesses in your background; such as, frequent job changes.

6. It provides an employer with topics to talk about during an interview and this can help you prepare for the interview and control part of the conversation.

7. It shows that you are professional and that you understand the needs of the job and the needs of the organization.

8. It provides proof that you are worth the money you hope to earn.

9. It whets the appetite of the interviewer, compelling him to want to learn more about you.

10. It answers the question "why should I hire you and what's in it for me?"

11. It demonstrates whether you have taken the time to research the company and tailored your resume to fit the position for which you are applying.

Anatomy of a Resume

A great resume has many different segments, each designed to support and showcase your unique skills, abilities and accomplishments. The way in which you arrange these segments will depend on the specific job and how you want the reader to draw his focus. The first five segments on this list should be included on every resume.

1. **Contact Information**– include your name, phone number(s), email address and professional website URL

2. **Professional Summary Statement** – this section must be compelling reading. It is an opportunity to position yourself and present your brand. Summarize your career as it relates to the position for which you are applying. Highlight your achievements and make sure to include related keywords

3. **Keywords and Skills** – include six to twelve technical and transferable skills related to the specific position

4. **Work/Professional Experience** - start with your last job, list your job title, company, location and dates of employment. Detail your work experience using action verbs and keywords. This section can take many forms including reverse chronological, functional, or combination resume styles

5. **Education and Training** – start with your formal academic education and qualifications. List professional courses you've taken, job related training and professional development

6. **Accreditations, Licenses, Publications, and Patents** – highlight key technical knowledge, abilities, and areas of expertise

7. **Honors and Awards** – detail your accomplishments, awards, and portfolio

8. **Professional Affiliations and Memberships** – list related groups and offices held

9. **Job Relevant Activities** – relate volunteer activities, interests and hobbies that highlight skills that are related to the job.

10. **Languages** – include the language, level of fluency, and knowledge

Keyword Tips

Keywords are company or industry specific words or phrases that reflect specific skills, abilities, and qualifications. Thousands of companies and recruiters screen resumes using scanning technology that electronically identifies keywords that match their specific hiring criteria. It is critical that the right keywords are included in your resume, cover letter, and other job search communications like LinkedIn, Facebook, etc.

1. Develop a list of keywords from your current and past experiences.

2. Take a close look at the job description of the targeted position. Keywords are usually more technical and specific to each job description. Look for words that are repeated several times and placed at the beginning of the "Duties" section.

3. If you do not have a job description, look for similar positions on job boards and the profiles of individuals you believe are qualified or have held positions that are similar to the one you are seeking.

4. Find the 6 -15 keywords listed in the job description and highlight or write them down. Many job seekers do not take the time to analyze the keywords and language used in the job posting.

5. Compare the job description and your list of keywords. Identify which of your keywords directly relate to the job description and analyze how your current skills can be transformed to fit the language of your targeted job. Matching transferable skills can be done with a set of carefully selected keywords. Here is an example: teaching = training = facilitating.

6. Integrate keywords into the "Professional Summary/ Summary of Qualifications" section at the top of your resume.

7. In addition to your resume, my recommendation is to add keywords to your cover letter and LinkedIn profile. Integrate keywords in all sections of your resume. A good goal is to have 20-35 keywords in your resume and use varying forms of the keyword. For example, use the keywords "manager" and "management". Remember, the scanning technology is programmed to identify specific keywords.

8. Add a special section of 6-15 keywords labeled "Key Skills," "Core Competencies," or "Areas of Expertise."

9. Use keywords to describe your work experiences.

10. Make sure to include keywords to highlight all of your accomplishments.

Transferable Skills

1. One of the most important things you can do in your job search is to clearly explain how your past experience relates to the position for which you are applying.

2. Bridge your past with your desired future by taking your skills and experience and express them in the industry language and terminology that fits the new job.

3. Transferable skills are skills acquired during any activity in your life; this includes jobs, classes, projects, parenting, hobbies, or sports

4. If you are seeking a job in the same field, portraying your transferable skills will be relatively easy. Research the company and specific job to know what skills to emphasize.

5. If you are changing careers, you may lack direct experience but think, "how can I portray this skill so that it supports the idea of doing what I want to do in my next career?" An example is: A teacher can use the same skill set to become a corporate trainer.

6. You can find transferable skills by reviewing job descriptions, job search websites, Occupational Informat Network (O'Net), or speaking with workers in your desired field.

7. The formula to identify transferable skills is: Old Job Skills > Skills Required for New Job (transferable) > Related Accomplishment

8. Examples of the general transferable skills that most employers are looking for include: communication skills, problem solving, leadership skills, teamwork, and ability to sell and persuade others.

9. Quantify your transferable skills by preparing examples of how you successfully used the transferable skills in your past experience

10. Transferable skills should appear in your cover letter, resume, and discussed during your interview.

Rules for Resumes

1. **Customize Your Resume**
   There is no one size fits all resume. Your resume needs to reflect the specific set of skills and qualifications the employer is looking for. Each time you send out a resume, it should be tailored for that specific employer and match the requirements of the job.

2. **Create a Resume Template**
   Your resume template will have the general sections that contain all your work history, skills, qualifications, and education. This will enable you to pull information into your resume from the template to create the customized resume when applying for specific opportunities. The template will allow you to easily shift the focus of your resume from one skill set to another without starting from scratch each time you send a resume.

3. **Create an Attention Grabbing Resume**
   The idea is to engage your reader visually so use lines, boxes, borders, shading, colors, charts and graphs if it will help your resume stand out in a good way. Do not use these special graphics if your resume is going to be scanned.

4. **Make it Easy to Read**
   Include enough information to whet your potential employer's appetite, but provide enough white space so that your resume is easy to read. Also, select a font and font size that is easy to read.

5. **Include LinkedIn**
   More than 80% of employers and recruiters will check your LinkedIn site before they consider contacting you. Make sure your LinkedIn URL is on your resume and your profile supports your brand.

6. **List the Most Important Information First**
   The most relevant information should be listed at the top of your resume. Each major section should begin with your most compelling points to hook your reader.

7. **Write Tight**
   Explain your work in vivid quantifiable language. Employers read through resumes very quickly so your sentences should be succinct and to the point without fluffy words or statements. Your accomplishments and awards should be listed as bullet points.

8. **Incorporate Relevant Keywords**
   Electronic scanning technology is used to identify company or industry specific words or phrases which reflect distinct skills, abilities and qualifications that match their particular hiring criteria. Read the job description and research the company's website for certain words and phrases that come up again and again. Those recurring words and phrases are keywords and should be incorporated in your resume.

9. **Convey Your Unique Value**
   Summarize your achievements in three to five sentences in the "Professional Summary/ Summary of Qualifications" section at the top of your resume.

10. **Length Does Matter**
    Think carefully about the details you need to include in your resume. Employers usually do not want to wade through a three or four page resume when a carefully arranged two page resume will suffice. There are some exceptions like Federal Resumes. If you have less than five years of experience, a one page resume will work nicely.

Resume Don'ts

Recruiters use resumes to screen potential candidates out. Including these items will deter you from being considered for your ideal position:

1. **Typos and grammatical errors** – Spelling errors and incorrect tenses lack professionalism. Have several people, who are good proofreaders, review your resume before sending it out to anyone.

2. **Salary requirements** – If requested, this information should be included in your cover letter. If stating your salary is a requirement, state your salary as a range.

3. **Personal information** - Marital status, number of children, health, and age should never be listed on a professional resume, period.

4. **Questionable e-mail address** – Employers will immediately question your professionalism when they see a cute or suggestive e-mail address like "hellokitty2@gmail.com" or "bigdaddy@gmail.com." Use your name as your e-mail address whenever possible.

5. **Ethnicity or national origin**

6. **References** – Stating the "references will be furnished upon request" is a waste of space. An employer will request this information if there is interest in you.

7. **Reasons for leaving previous jobs** - Having been fired, laid-off, sexually harassed, or not getting along with your boss or co-workers has no business on a resume because it is not a confessional.

8. **Date availability for employment** – Unless you are graduating from high school, college or university, most employers expect you to begin employment two to three weeks after an offer has been accepted.

9. **Never lie** – Do not make up a job, degree or an experience you did not have. Most employers conduct a background check to validate the information you provide on your resume. You can get fired long after you are hired for having false information listed on your resume.

10. **Cluttered Appearance** – Appearance does count. Your resume should have a clean, polished, professional look. Just because you have access to 50 different fonts and sizes does not mean you have to use them. Be consistent in your use of fonts, size, spacing, and allow for plenty of white space to enhance readability.

Why Use a Chronological Resume

1. This is the most common and widely accepted resume format used

2. Employers and recruiters prefer it because it is simple, straight forward, and easy to scan

3. The "Work/Professional Experience" section should start with your last job, lists your job title, company, location, and dates of employment

4. Jobs are listed in reverse chronological order from your most recent to your earliest job detailing your work experience using action verbs, keywords, and quantifiable data

5. Enables interviewer to easily ask questions about your job performance, upward mobility, and allows you to easily tell your story

6. Should be used by those with a strong consistent work history who demonstrate a logical progression in responsibilities in the same line of work

7. This is the preferred format in industries that value tradition and formality; such as, Banking, Accounting and Law

8. Employers are easily able to determine your work performance at each company

9. Use this type of resume if you have worked for top tier employers in your field with name recognition and a positive image

10. Should not be used if you are switching careers, have gaps in employment, or lack experience in the field you are pursuing

Advantages of a Functional Resume

1. Highlights your skills, accomplishments, and qualifications rather than chronological work history

2. The main heading consists of functions or skills. Responsibilities, accomplishments, and quantifiable achievements are described under each function or skill

3. Use if you want to transition to a new career, have gaps in employment, re-entering the workforce, or frequent job changes

4. Use if you have very diverse experiences that don't add up to a clear career path

5. Showcases relevant experience that has been unpaid; such as, volunteer work and college activities

6. Works for job seekers who have performed activities in their past jobs and want to avoid looking over qualified

7. This format will help emphasize transferable skills when looking to change careers

8. Details your skills as they match the requirements of a specific position for which you are applying by including relevant achievements and accomplishments

9. Enables you to more readily accentuate soft skills

10. Allows you to customize your resume for a specific job

Tips for Uploading Your Resume

Whether you upload your resume to a job board or company website, you can expect that they use an Applicant Tracking Systems (ATS) to find the best candidates for a job. The ATS is used to scan, sort, and rank the resumes of suitable candidates. Here are some basic rules to follow to ensure your resume will pass through the filtering software.

1. Choose the most applicable job specific key words for your career field and arrange them in appropriate order. If you have the job description, select the key words that appear most often and apply to you.

2. Use a popular, common font such as Arial, Cambia, New Times Roman, or Helvetica to ensure optimum readability.

3. Use a font size between 10 points and 14 points.

4. Avoid italics, script, and underlining passages.

5. Avoid graphics and shading. Do not use reverse boxes to print white type on a black background. Scanners cannot read them and the information in the box will appear as if it is missing from your resume.

6. Use horizontal and vertical lines sparingly and allow a quarter inch of white space around them.

7. Text based resumes are the preferred format for submitting resumes electronically because they retain their formatting consistently across computer programs and platforms.

8. The file must be in a common format such as Word, .DOC., .TXT, etc. to comply with the instructions. Avoid using compressed files. Be aware of your file size. Usually, your document should be no larger than 1000KB and less than five pages long.

9. When converting your word document for uploading, scroll through the entire document to make sure that the information has been converted correctly into the database.

10. Follow the instructions to upload your resume on each site because they do vary. Some sites may instruct you to copy and paste the text from your resume into a blank field on their webpage. Others want you to use built-in resume features where you may have to enter information in specific sections.

11. Confirm that your resume has been uploaded successfully.

Checklist for Writing Your Federal Resume

1. Focus your resume to target one occupational series at a time. This can be done by changing your profile statement.

2. It must contain your "Knowledge, Skills and Abilities Statements" (KSA) within the body of your resume.

3. Highlight the specialized experience that directly relates to the one occupational series.

4. Add keywords, 10-20 keywords, which are listed in the "Mission," "Duties" and "Qualifications" sections of the vacancy announcement.

5. List your most relevant experience on the first page.

6. Be detailed about your experience. Give specific examples and quantify your accomplishments and examples (when possible) in the "Specialized Experience" section.

7. Be sure to include the announcement number, title, and grade of the job for which you are applying.

8. Read and follow instructions including all required documents requested.

9. Use a recognized resume format, either Outline Format or USAJOBS format.

10. Expect your resume to be 3-6 pages in length.

THE INTERVIEW

A job interview is not a test of your knowledge, but your ability to use it at the right time.

    Unknown

I can count on one hand the number of people who wrote me a thank you note after having an interview, and I gave almost all of them jobs.

    Kate Roardon

The Interview

1. How to Nail the Information Interview
2. Your Interview Tool Kit
3. Phone interview Tips
4. Video Interviewing
5. How Do I Fill This Thing Out: Tips to Quickly and Professionally Complete a Job Application
6. Women – Put Your Best Foot Forward
7. Men – Put Your Best Foot Forward
8. Interview Attire Don'ts
9. Important Things to Do Before the Interview
10. Quick Tips to Ace Your Interview
11. Ways to Botch an interview
12. Employers Really Want to Know
13. Winning interview Strategies
14. Mastering the Behavior/Situational Interview
15. Signs Your Interview is Going Well
16. Signs Your Interview is Not Going Well
17. Questions to Ask Yourself After the Interview
18. Do You Know What Your References Are Saying About You?
19. Thank you Letter Tips

The Interview

20. The Follow-up Phone Call

21. Salary Negotiation Tips

22. Make a Smooth Transition to Your New Job

How to Nail the Informational Interview

The informational interview is one of the best ways to get information, expand your network, and receive leads for new career opportunities. This may be the easiest interview you will ever have; but to do it correctly takes a little preparation. There is an art to conducting a good informational interview. Here is how you finesse your next informational interview:

1. After identifying the career or company you want to learn more about, look for people in those areas. How can you find those people? Start by asking family, friends, ex-coworkers, and members of organizations to which you belong. Your LinkedIn network, school alumni office, and trade associations are avenues you should also use. It is much easier to secure a "yes" from someone you want to interview if you are able to use a name of someone that they know.

2. Keep it short by requesting only 15 minutes of their time. You want to request a reasonable amount of time which is not a burden or imposition to their busy schedule.

3. The most important part of your preparation is to develop good questions. Research the organization and occupation and have basic knowledge about your interest.

4. The questions you prepare should help you learn if this is the type of job you are prepared to do and whether you will enjoy it. You also want to ask specific questions about job tasks, working conditions, and career preparation.

5. Develop open ended questions which will allow the person to do most of the talking.

6. You may also want to prepare a resume to bring to the interview. The person you interview may ask about your experience and education. Your resume will give them a snapshot of your background and allows them to give you more relevant advice or suggestions to improve your resume.

7. Dress as if you were interviewing for a job at that company. Be sure to bring a notepad and pen, your resume and business cards. Make sure you arrive on-time, but no more than 15 minutes before your appointment.

8. You are there to <u>gather</u> information, so don't ask them what you should do with your life or career and do not ask for a job! Ask the questions you have developed listen and take notes. Allow the person you are interviewing to do most of the talking.

9. Be respectful of the interviewer's time, monitor and end the interview when you said you would. Of course, it is ok to spend more time if the interviewee wants to continue.

10. Always end the interview by thanking the person and asking two important questions. Can you suggest other people I can speak to and may I mention your name when I speak to them? The answers to these questions can lead to your next informational interview.

Bonus Tips:

11. Send a thank you note to the person you interviewed after the interview. Report back to them if you have followed up on any suggestions. By building rapport with these contacts, you increase the likelihood that they will offer assistance with your job search.

12. Take a moment to record your thoughts about the occupation and workplace. What did you like? What concerns surfaced? What advice did you receive? Do you think this is the occupation or company you would like to pursue?

13. It is important not to base your decision on one individual. You should conduct a few interviews to confirm any ideas or opinions before you make a final decision.

Your Interview Tool Kit

These are the indispensable items you should take to every interview. They will help you complete job applications and/or can be used during the interview:

1. Resume

2. List of references

3. List of transferable skills

4. List of questions to ask

5. List of previous employers including addresses, phone numbers, and contact names

6. Awards and recognitions

7. Sample of projects/portfolio

8. Copies of performance reviews

9. Directions to the interview location

10. Notepad and pen

Phone Interview Tips

The telephone interview is an opportunity to gain an in-person interview. These tips will help you make the most of your phone interview.

1. Know your resume thoroughly. The sole purpose of the phone interview is to narrow down the pool of applicants to a few candidates. To move to the next round of interviews, you must respond appropriately to questions that verify the information on your resume and determine if you have the basic qualifications for the job.

2. Practice basic interview questions and your phone technique with someone who is willing to give you honest constructive feedback.

3. Schedule an appointment for a telephone interview so you can be prepared and free from distractions.

4. Find a quiet spot away from noise and distractions. Use a phone that has the clearest reception. Make sure the dog is not barking or the neighbor's lawnmower is not taking away from your conversation.

5. Smile and use your voice to convey enthusiasm. Use vocal variety while answering the interviewer's questions. The recruiter cannot see your face or cue into your body language, so it is important for your voice to convey your personality.

6. Relax

7. Have your *interview tool kit* in front of you for easy reference.

8. Record the interviewer's name, title, phone number, company name, address, and points discussed during the interview.

9. Take notes just as long as it does not distract from your conversation. Take advantage of the fact that the interviewer cannot see what you are doing.

10. Write the interviewer a thank you note.

Video Interviewing

Video interviewing is primarily used in place of a phone interview as part of the pre-screening process. Companies are moving toward this form of interviewing to save time and money. Here's how to prepare:

1. Make sure you know how to work the technology (computer, tablet, or chat system) and/or have the required downloaded application or plug-in in place. You will be much more relaxed and able to concentrate on the actual interview instead of worrying about the technical set-up of the equipment. Don't be afraid to ask for help or additional instructions if you are unsure.

2. Eliminate any background noise in the interview area. The microphone will pick up sounds you may be accustom to, but will be distracting to the interviewer. Be aware of ticking clocks, drumming your fingers, or tapping the pen on the desk.

3. Check your physical surroundings to make sure you have good lighting. There is nothing worse than sitting in the shadows or looking like you are in an interrogation room. Check for any physical distractions which include disorganized or messy surroundings, people walking back and forth.

4. Set your computer up early and log on, as soon as possible, to make sure you have a good connection. Test the internet speed, microphone and speaker volume to ensure you come across loud and clear. Your electronic device should be fully charged or plugged in because video can quickly drain your battery.

5. Dress just like you are attending an in-person interview. Wear the same type professional attire you would wear if you were going to interview with the hiring manager at a company.

6. Look into the camera as you are answering the questions. Looking away from the camera or down at the desk will make it appear that you are distracted, unprepared, you have something to hide, or all three.

7. Use more non-verbal cues during your interview such as nodding your head in agreement. Make sure the expression on your face and your upper body language reflect a positive and professional image.

8. Practice your video interview with someone to determine how you come across on camera.

9. Be completely prepared and situated before the interview begins. Remember, this is very similar to an in-person interview. The interviewer will be able to detect if you are reading your responses, shuffling papers, or looking at notes.

10. Be confident! The interviewer is able to record and play back your responses to the same set of interview questions asked of every other candidate. You will standout because with these tips, you have prepared specifically for the video interview.

How Do I Fill This Thing Out?
Tips to Quickly and Professionally Complete a Job Application

1. Whether on line or in person, it is important to have all the information you will need to complete the application readily available. The items needed are listed in the "Your Interview Tool Kit" (see page 66) in this section. This information should be organized in a neat professional manner.

2. Complete a practice application. This will help you write a brief, coherent, and impressive description of the work you have performed for each job. It will also reduce the time needed to complete the final application and allow the application to look neat and professional.

3. Write neatly with a black or blue pen.

4. When applying in person:
   - Look professional by dressing appropriately; you never know who will be observing you.
   - Make sure you are well groomed; hair, nails, jewelry, and accessories are in good taste.
   - Ask to complete an employment application in a professional, friendly, yet confident manner.
   - Be prepared for an "on the spot" interview.
   - Be professional and polite to everyone, especially the receptionist.
   - Try to engage the manager or receptionist by asking an intelligent question or by making a business comment. You are more likely to be remembered and called back.

5. Allow at least 15-30 minutes to complete an application.

6. Follow the directions on the application. If a question or section does not apply to you, write "N/A" which means not applicable. The employer will know you read the complete application and did not ignore or skip any sections.

7. Employers try to weed out applicants as soon as possible. Be prepared to complete a questionnaire directly related to basic skills needed for the position for which you are applying. These questionnaires cover areas such as basic math, customer service skills, and ethics questions.

8. Review the application before submitting it. Check for any spelling errors.

9. You will also be required to sign the application to confirm the accuracy of the information submitted. Make sure you tell the truth on your application! Be aware that employees have been fired for "inaccuracies" uncovered on their application.

10. Follow-up by calling the company in a week to check the status of your application.

Women - Put Your Best Foot Forward

Determine the appropriate dress code for the company culture and industry in which you are interviewing. Be aware that many companies have a business casual dress code. To make a good first impression, may require a visit to the company prior to your interview to observe what the employees are wearing. Even if the employees of an organization dress casually on the job, dress up for the interview unless you are specifically told otherwise by the employer.

1. Keep makeup to a minimum.

2. Nails should be neat and clean with neutral or clear colored finger nail polish. Nails should not be excessively long.

3. In a traditional business setting, choose a suit that is conservative in navy blue, black, gray, or neutral colors. In a business casual setting, choose a nice skirt or pair of slacks and coordinating jacket in conservative colors mentioned above.

4. In a traditional business setting, wear closed or peep toe shoes that compliment your outfit and accessories. Moderate looking shoes can be worn in a business casual setting. (Never stilettos or flip flops).

5. Select a soft colored blouse or sweater in a non-see through material that coordinates with your skirt or pants, and jacket.

6. Carry a small simple purse along with a portfolio. You may choose to carry a small brief case or business-like tote in place of a purse.

7. Wear minimal jewelry. Remember less is best!

8. Wear pantyhose or stockings with all outfits.

9. Have a neat, clean, professional hairstyle.

10. Wear minimal perfume or cologne

Men - Put Your Best Foot Forward

In the first few seconds of an interview, the interviewer will form an initial opinion about you based on your appearance. During an interview, your attire should confirm your professionalism and support your goal of obtaining a job. So, dress appropriately for the position you are seeking. In general, this means erring on the side of a conservative or classic look.

1. In a traditional business setting, choose a suit that is conservative in navy blue, black, gray, or neutral colors. A white, ivory, or light blue shirt and conservative silk tie should coordinate with your suit.

2. In a business casual setting, choose a nice pair of pants and coordinating jacket in the conservative colors mentioned above. A polo shirt or a shirt with a collar should be worn with your business casual outfit.

3. Make sure your shoes are <u>polished.</u>

4. Your belt and shoes should be in a matching color.

5. Wear dark colored over the calf socks.

6. Your face should be clean-shaven, or beard and mustache should be trimmed and neat.

7. Go light on the after shave and cologne.

8. Wear a conservative watch.

9. Nails should be neat and clean.

10. Carry a portfolio or small briefcase.

Interview Attire <u>Don'ts</u>

You should stand out from your competition based on your knowledge, skills, and abilities. Your interpersonal skills and ability to respond to questions in an intelligent and well thought out manner are the most important factors during an interview. You should not be remembered for your bad interview attire.

1. Flip flops or sneakers
2. T-shirts and shorts
3. Too much jewelry
4. Jeans
5. Pants that are too tight or too low rise
6. Blouses or tops that show too much cleavage or your stomach
7. Underwear should not show - That means bras, bra straps (even if they match), thongs, briefs and boxers should not show
8. Skirts that are too short
9. Ill-fitting clothes
10. Sunglasses perched on top of your head or worst, worn during an interview

Bonus Tips:

11. Overly bright or wild patterns, unless you are applying for a job in the fashion sector
12. Tattoos and piercings
13. Bare legs or patterned hose
14. Unusual hair colors or hair styles
15. Wrinkled, stained or dirty clothes

Important Things to Do Before the Interview

1. Review the information about the company and prepare three to six questions to ask the interviewer during the interview process.

2. Practice and review responses to the most commonly asked and anticipated interview questions.

3. Know the specific location of your interview and have directions to get to your location.

4. Arrive 10 – 15 minutes early for your interview.

5. Be aware that your interview begins when you enter the company's parking lot.

6. Treat all staff members (especially the receptionist) in a professional and respectful manner. Know who will be interviewing you and ask for them when you enter the building.

7. Your mobile phone and other electronic devices should be silenced or turned off before entering the building.

8. Be prepared to complete an application. Use the information in "Your Interview Tool Kit" (see page 66) to help you fill out your application quickly.

9. Make sure your interview clothes are clean and pressed.

10. Get a good night's sleep.

Quick Tips to Ace Your Interview

1. Give a firm handshake… not a wimpy one

2. Sit down only after you have been asked

3. Don't place items on the interviewer's desk. This is considered an invasion of their personal space

4. Relax; assist the interviewer in getting the interview going

5. Make frequent eye contact with the interviewer during the interview especially while answering questions

6. Convey interest and enthusiasm

7. Maintain open and positive body language and occasional verbal acknowledgement

8. Be responsive

9. Remember the interview is not a confessional nor a social outing

10. Don't chew gum or candy

Bonus Tips:

11. If you are involved in a lunch interview, order food that is easy to eat and will allow you to talk. The main purpose of the meeting is to sell your skills and abilities…not to feed you

12. Listen carefully to the information the recruiter is providing

13. Ask questions about training programs and other information relevant to what the interviewer says

14. Share knowledge about the company from your research

15. Present a positive image of your skills and area of knowledge that match the job requirements

16. Share your strengths and assets

17. Be ready to define long and short term goals

18. Determine the steps necessary for further consideration

19. Ask for a business card or write down the name of each person who talks with you. Make sure you have their correct title and spelling of their names, as well as, the email and address of the interviewer

20. Leave the interviewer with a positive impression

Ways to Botch an Interview

1. Bring your friends or, better yet, your parents to the interview; they can certainly vouch for your character.

2. Wear the sweat stained, wrinkled white shirt with the dirty collar to the interview.

3. Forget the interviewer's name and compensate by calling him/her "Honey, Sugar, Cupcake, or Chief."

4. When asked "Tell me about yourself," in response, you start with your earliest childhood memories and finish with your most recent divorce.

5. Let the interviewer know you are important. Interrupt the interview by taking phone calls and responding to text messages.

6. When answering questions, refer to yourself in the third person, for example, "Fred is very comfortable with public speaking and makes presentations with enthusiasm and self-confidence."

7. To show why you want the job, mention that you have a house payment, two car payments, and three kids to feed.

8. Make no eye contact during the interview and diligently make copious notes on your electronic device.

9. Answer interview questions with as few words as possible, after all, everything they need to know about you is on your resume.

10. Can't answer a question? Change the subject and create your own rambling answer; maybe, the interviewer won't notice.

Bonus Tips:

11. Talk about how awful it is to work at your current place of employment and explain how you must be the most unlucky person to have a string of bozos and jerks as your past supervisors.

12. Yawn or appear disinterested in the interview.

13. Be completely uninformed about the company; ask, "What does the company do?"

14. Ask the interviewer personal questions; for example: "Are you married," "What are you doing after this interview," or "Can we go out for a drink?"

15. Don't smile. Giving the interviewer a cold stone stare with an impatient glare after difficult questions are asked.

16. Either give the interviewer a wet, cold or limp handshake, or a bone crushing grip.

17. Ask questions that indicate you were not listening during the interview or ask only about salary, benefits, vacation, and company recognized holidays.

18. Don't ask any questions at all.

19. Secretly (or so you think), record the interview. How else are you going to remember what you said and what went right or wrong.

20. Lie about your duties and responsibilities. The interviewer has no way of knowing whether you managed that project or not.

Employers Really Want to Know

The last thing you want to do is look foolish and unprepared in front of an interviewer, but with so many different interview questions, knowing how to respond to them can be a daunting task! It helps to understand the kinds of questions you might be asked and know what the interviewer is trying to find out so you can work out the best way to answer them. Interviewers want to know:

1. **If you prepared for the interview**
   Tell me about yourself?
   What are your strengths?
   What are your weaknesses?
   Answering these questions is usually your first hurdle. Most people think they can answer these common interview questions but stumble immediately because they have not prepared the right answers to these questions. Prepare responses that are specifically designed for the job for which you are interviewing.

2. **If you are qualified for the position**
   What were your responsibilities in your last position?
   Give me examples of ideas or projects you have implemented.
   These questions enable the interviewer to get to know you beyond what is written in your resume and specific to your past work and educational experience.

3. **What motivates you**
   What are you looking for in career development?
   What personal accomplishment are you most proud of?
   Why do you want to leave your current position?
   The interviewer wants to gain some deeper insight into your personality and determine if your interests are compatible with this type of job.

4. **If you have any negatives**
   Tell me one thing about yourself that you don't want me to know.
   What two positive traits will your boss/coworkers say you don't have?
   No one is perfect. These questions force you to be humble but *give* an opportunity to relate an incident from which you learned

an important lesson. The interviewer wants to hear about a problem area you have worked on and improved.

5. **If you are a good fit**
   Describe a decision you made that was unpopular and how did you handle implementing it?
   What assignment was difficult for you and how did you resolve the issue?
   The theory behind these questions is that your past behavior will predict your future behavior. This line of questions delves more into your soft skills, your ability to work with and through people, and your problem solving abilities. How you respond will determine if there is a fit between your skills and the position the company is seeking to fill.

6. **If you can handle pressure**
   Sell me this pen.
   What animal best describes your management style?
   How do you handle tension with your boss?
   These questions are designed to determine how you react under stress or handle surprises in a business situation. If you encounter a stress question, your best bet is to stay calm, diplomatic, and positive in your response. Answer the question to the best of your ability.

7. **If you want their job with their company**
   Why should we hire you?
   How will you complement this department?
   What would you do if one of our competitors offered you a position?
   The interviewer is trying to determine whether you are truly interested in the industry and company. Prepare answers that show you believe in the products or services of the company and reinforce that your interests are compatible with this particular job.

8. **If you can satisfy their needs or solve their problems**
   This department has a fast paced environment
   The last employee was promoted to...
   There has been turnover in this department....

These statements alert you to what the company is looking for. It is your job to provide them with quantifiable information that you are the answer to their problem or need.

9. **If you have supervisory or management potential**
   What do you think are the most important aspects of supervision?
   Describe your management style.
   Some companies have a preferred management style. Answer the questions in a positive manner describing your interpersonal skills and how you incorporate them when working with others. Give specific examples of your ability to apply these skills.

10. **If you can contribute to the company**
    Tell me about a contribution you've made to a team.
    Tell me about a major accomplishment.
    If hired today, what would you accomplish first?
    These questions are designed to determine if you have initiative and how your past contributions can translate into success for the company. Give them proof, use specific examples to demonstrate that you delivered more than expected.

Winning Interview Strategies

Your resume may have impressed the recruiter enough to get you an interview. However, there are several things that can make or break your chances of getting hired for the job. Even when you know how to respond to the questions, interviews can be awkward or downright disastrous without having some strategies. Here are some tips to help put the interview puzzle together.

1. **Start with your resume**
   You must know and be prepared to explain everything on your resume. Determine which skills, projects, and accomplishments you want to highlight in each position listed on your resume. Tie these skills and abilities from your previous positions to the job for which you are interviewing. Be ready to explain why you left each position and any gaps in your employment.

2. **Find out what the interviewer is looking for**
   Ask the interviewer to describe their ideal candidate. Listen for skills and abilities and how your skills and attributes relate and transfer. It is up to you to describe your skills and abilities in a way to allow the interviewer to understand the clear connection.

3. **Prepare to ask good questions**
   There is nothing worse than interviewing a candidate who does not ask questions. It shows a lack of preparation, imagination and initiative. This is your opportunity to engage the interviewer in a two way conversation, so be prepared to ask at least two to four well formulated questions. This is a good time to show that you have done research about the company and that you were listening to what your interviewer has said. Design questions that include some facts or figures to show that you have taken the time to think about the company/or this new position. You can also ask questions that piggy back on something that the interviewer might have mentioned about the company or position earlier in the interview.

4. **Check your body language**

   Most interviewers closely monitor your verbal and non-verbal cues during an interview to determine your interest in the job, comfort level, and if you are telling the truth. During your interview sit up straight, lean slightly forward in your chair and maintain a pleasant expression to project interest and enthusiasm. Make frequent eye contact with the interviewer especially while answering the questions. In a difficult situation we often fold our hands across our bodies to help us feel secure. It is better not to do this because it comes across as defensive. Maintain open body language by keeping your hands relaxed in your lap. Refrain from fidgeting, shaking your foot, playing with your hair, rocking back and forth, or any other nervous behaviors.

5. **A little silence can be golden**

   It is alright to briefly pause to process a question; however, if you don't understand a question seek clarification by paraphrasing. Paraphrase the question to make sure you are answering the right question and to help frame your response. This will also buy you time to think about the question if you do not have an answer formulated right away.

6. **Keep your cool**

   Have some standard phrases memorized such as "Let me think about that question for a second" or "That's a good question" which will allow you to respond positively to surprise or aggressive questions.

7. **Ask the hard question**

   Ask the interviewer if he has any further questions about your skills, abilities or attributes. If he does, answer each question thoughtfully. This is your opportunity to remove any objections or questions about you being the ideal candidate.

8. **Have a strong close**

   Let the interviewer know you want this job! You want to make one final attempt to prove you are the best candidate for the job. You do this by summarizing your skills and attributes as they relate to the position and organization, telling the interviewer that you are very interested in the position.

9. **Ask about the next steps**
At the end of your close, ask about the next steps. At this point, you should have a good idea about your chances of moving forward in the interview process.

10. **Practice, practice and practice again**
Practice your responses and strong close out loud in front of a mirror. Make sure you are able to maintain good eye contact and have a pleasant expression on your face. Review your responses enough so that you exude confidence and enthusiasm. Knowing what you will say will also eliminate the temptation to use filler words such as "uh," "ah," and "you know." Solicit the help from a friend who will give you honest constructive feedback and ask them to conduct a mock interview with you.

Mastering the Behavioral/Situational Interview

Behavioral interview questions are based on the skills required for that position. Instead of asking how you <u>will</u> handle a situation, the employer wants to know how you handled a situation in the past. An example of a behavioral/situational question is: "Describe a decision you made that was unpopular and how you implemented it?" It is based on the idea that the best predictor of your behavior in the future is explaining how you have handled the same or similar situation in the past. So, how do you prepare for behavioral interview questions? Here are some tips:

1. Review the job description to determine what type of skills the interviewer is looking for.

2. Prepare several stories that illustrate or demonstrate the skills and characteristics the employer is seeking from reading the job responsibilities and qualifications.

3. Your stories should be constructed to make you stand out from the other candidates who may have been interviewed.

4. Make sure you have a different story to explain each important skill in the job description.

5. Your stories should be recent; within the last three years, if possible, and can involve work and non-work related experiences.

6. The examples provided should center on <u>your</u> actions and contributions. Your answers should include the words "I, me and my" rather than "We, they and us."

7. Keep in mind that the employer is looking for a detailed and succinct response. Use the STAR method to help you structure a response that includes all the important information to answer the question. **STAR** stands for:
    - **S**ituation – A specific situation.
    - **T**ask – The task that needed to be done
    - **A**ction – The action you took
    - **R**esults – The results or what happened

8. Limit the time it takes to explain your examples. Each example should take no more than one to three minutes and paint a clear picture of the situation, otherwise you risk rambling and losing the interviewer's interest.

9. Practice telling your stories until you are fluid, detailed, concise, and complete.

10. There are no perfect responses. However, how you respond will determine if there is a good fit between your skills and the position the company is seeking to fill.

Signs Your Interview is Going Well

1. Your interview is scheduled for one hour but you are interviewed for an hour and a half.

2. The interviewer gives you a tour of the office and introduces you to the members of the team.

3. Interviewer gives you reinforcing feedback to your interview responses.

4. Interviewer explains next steps of the interviewing process before you ask.

5. You are asked for your list of references and the company conducts your pre-employment background check.

6. The interviewer's facial expressions and body language are positive.

7. Your next interview is with the head of the department.

8. After a positive interview, you are asked about tentative start dates.

9. The interviewer talks salary.

10. Human resources is re-involved in hiring process.

Signs Your Interview is Not Going Well

1. Your interview is scheduled for four hours but your interviewer cuts the interview short and sends you home after the first hour.

2. The interviewer does not smile at you after the initial introduction and pleasantries.

3. The interviewer is distracted or interrupts the interview (unless it is an absolute emergency.)

4. The interviewer continues to ask disqualifying questions such as "Do you think you will get bored with this position?" "Do you think you are over qualified for this position?"

5. You cannot formulate a concrete answer to two or more questions.

6. There is no mention about the next steps in the interview process or no verbal confirmation that you will continue to the next round of interviews.

7. The interviewer's body language is negative, for example; hands are crossed, no direct eye contact, and body is turned away from you.

8. There is no spark or commonality between you and the interviewer.

9. Your interview responses are challenged and/or there are no follow-up questions asked after you respond to a question.

10. The interviewer **will not** give you his contact information so that you may follow-up.

Questions to Ask Yourself After the Interview

1. How did the interview go?

2. What points did I make that seemed to interest the employer?

3. Did I present my qualifications well? Did I overlook any that were pertinent to the job?

4. Did I pass up clues for the best way to "sell" myself?

5. Did I learn all I need to know about the job? Or did I forget or hesitate to ask about factors that were important to me?

6. Did I talk too much? Too little?

7. Did I interview the employer rather than permit the employer to interview me?

8. Was I too tense?

9. Was I too aggressive? Not aggressive enough?

10. How can I improve my next interview?

Do You Know What Your References Are Saying About You?

Your references are the people who vouch for your character and confirm the skills and abilities that you have so carefully described during the interview process. It is important that you take time to select and prepare your references. Unfortunately, many candidates give little thought and put forth minimal effort when listing their references.

1. **Choose your references carefully**
   Don't underestimate the importance of a good reference. Make sure you have three to five references from your past employment. Some companies want personal references, but usually the best references are direct supervisors and people who have seen your work first hand.

2. **Ask your choices if they will serve as references**
   It is bad manners to put someone down on your list of references without checking first to see if it is OK. This protects your interest in a couple of ways; you are able to confirm that they will speak positively about you and this will enable you to refresh their memory about your personality and performance.

3. **Select a reference who is enthusiastic and well spoken**
   If a reference clams up or acts aloof, the hiring manager may jump to the conclusion that he's withholding bad news because he fears legal repercussions.

4. **Provide your references with a copy of your resume**
   Give every reference a copy of your resume so that that person has information on the dates and places you worked. Don't make your reference have to do homework. Few people can remember exactly when you worked for the company or how long.

5. **Let your references know when a potential employer may be calling them**

6. **Coach your references on what to say about you if a potential employer calls**
   Provide anyone who agrees to be your reference with a short list of qualities/traits that you think are your strengths. If you list creativity, site projects that you came up with and how these impacted the company's bottom line. If you list leadership, recap your position of authority and how this impacted the company's bottom line. If you know that certain traits are of special interest to a company, inform your reference and ask him to emphasize that particular trait. Give your reference a specific example to share with the reference checker.

7. **Keep your reference contact information current**
   Make sure the contact information for each reference is current. Failure to update your reference list makes you look lazy or suspicious. You want the hiring manager to believe you are capable and thorough.

8. **Stamp out bad references**
   If you get someone's permission to list him as a reference but you still have reservations about what he will say about you, get a friend to make a phone call, pretending to be an employer who wants to know about your job history. Take no chances that someone you have listed will make negative or less than enthusiastic comments. A little paranoia can be healthy.

9. **Think ahead**
   Prepare a list of references on a separate piece of paper. When asked, you will be able to provide this information during an interview (this is part of your resume kit).

10. **Be prepared to explain**
    If you do not list your most recent supervisor, an interviewer may ask you "why not?" during the interview. It is smart to be prepared to answer that question.

Thank You Letter Tips

The best way to follow-up on an interview is to simply send a thank-you note to the interviewer. Surprisingly, fewer than twenty percent of the people who go on a job interview send a note thanking the interviewer for taking the time to speak with them.
A thank you note serves several purposes:

1. It shows that you are professional and that you truly appreciate the opportunity to be interviewed.

2. It also serves to remind the interviewer, several days after the interview, that you are a candidate for the position and that you still want the job.

3. It gives you an opportunity to mention any key points that you forgot to bring up during the interview.

4. It lets you answer any questions that you were not able to answer during the interview.

5. Plus, it gives you another opportunity to call the interviewer and convince her/him to give you a chance.

6. Remember, a thank you note should be written, not e-mailed, to everyone who interviewed you. E-mail a thank you note only when an interviewer specifies that this is the preferred means of communication.

7. To write a winning thank you letter include the following points:
    - Begin by thanking the interviewer and saying how much you enjoyed meeting him or her.
    - Tell the interviewer how excited you are by the prospect of working in the target position at this particular company.
    - Review the interview highlights and your strengths as they relate to the position.

8. Establish closure: Based on the conversation during the interview, reiterate your understanding of when you expect to hear from the employer again.

9. Proof read your letter to make sure it is free of punctuation and grammatical errors. Pay close attention to the correct titles and spelling of names.

10. Send your thank you letter within the first 48 hours after your interview.

The Follow-up Phone Call

Another way to show your interest in working at a company is to follow-up with a phone call. With a thank you note and a follow-up phone call, you are demonstrating that you really want the job. Use these tips as your guide.

1. Contact the interviewer by phone four to eight days after the interviewer has received your thank-you letter.

2. Don't assume people remember you when you call. Refresh their memory every time by putting yourself in context. "This is Jane, we met last week about the director's position.

3. Ask about the status of the position for which you interviewed and if you are still being considered.

4. If you are still in the running for the job, restate your interest in the position. Managers prefer to hire people who really want the job because people who really want the job tend to stay with the company longer, and put in a better effort.

5. If your call goes to voice mail, be prepared to leave a professional message. State you are doing a follow-up call on your interview and make sure you leave your phone number.

6. Limit your follow-ups to no more than once a week.

7. Give the recruiter/hiring manager a chance to call you back.

8. If you haven't heard from the recruiter by the time he said he would contact you, it is okay to call him.

9. Don't take a lack of communication personally.

10. Make sure you continue to job hunt and interview until you receive a suitable job offer. When you depend too much on one interview, you could be disappointed if you are not offered a job. In addition, you will have lost time and the possibility of securing other job interview opportunities. Continue to job hunt until a firm job offer has been made.

Salary Negotiation Tips

If you don't ask you will never receive a higher salary; yes, it requires courage, research, and practice. Here are some things to keep in mind.

1. **Don't be the first to show your hand** – Most professional organizations will give a salary range for the position in the early stages of the interview process because most hiring managers do not want to waste their time on someone whose salary expectations are too high or unrealistic. If they do not tell you; ask! Remember, you need to research the salary in your industry and geographic location before you speak. If the recruiter insists on you stating a salary, give the salary range you have researched.

2. **Ask for time** – After an initial offer has been made, ask for time to think about the offer. Request a follow-up conversation 24-48 hours after the offer. This allows you time to determine if this is a reasonable offer and build a strategy for asking for a higher salary or additional non-cash perks.

3. **Research salaries in your field** – look at recent salary survey information from websites such as: Salary.com, Guidestar.com, or Salaryexpert.com. Remember that salaries differ by geographic location, so be sure to factor that into your calculations.

4. **Experience does count** – Most companies have an established salary range for each position. Base your salary negotiations on the number of recent years of experience you have in that position. If you are just starting out in that field, expect to be offered a salary below the midpoint of that job salary range. If you have many years of experience, negotiate to be paid at the mid-point or higher.

5. **Your personal situation doesn't count** – Your expensive house and car, or child in college does not matter unless you are asked to relocate. Stick to your skills and the contributions you can make or problems you will solve as you begin to build your case.

6. **Prepare your case** – Talk about what you will do to earn the salary you are requesting. Will your skills and experience help streamline processes, reduce costs, increase sales, or lead to a larger customer base? Include salary research based on your experience and your position.

7. **Think "compensation package"** – In addition to your salary, there are other items to negotiate. Ask for additional vacation days, a sign-on bonus, an early or accelerated performance review cycle which will lead to more merit increases sooner, a bonus based on performance, additional education and training opportunities, an equity stake in the company, paid parking, or a gas card.

8. **What is your magic number?** – You should know what salary and compensation package you are willing to accept before entering into a final conversation with your future employer. In any good negotiation, you want to achieve a win-win situation, so very rarely does anyone get everything requested.

9. **Get it in writing** –Salary and anything else you have successfully negotiated need to be put in your final offer letter.

10. **Be Flexible** – You want to start your new relationship with a new employer on a positive note. You want to come across as pleasant and reasonable. You can ask for anything, but demand nothing!

Make a Smooth Transition to Your New Job

Starting a new job is exciting and daunting at the same time. You are leaving behind a familiar environment where you know how to play by the rules. Your manager and co-workers know your skills, abilities, and how fabulous you really are! Now, you are starting a new job in unfamiliar territory where there are new relationships you must form and new expectations to be met. Here are a few tips to make a smooth transition.

1. Do a "dry run" before you start work
There is nothing worse than being late on your first day of work. If you are going to drive, get up and out during the approximate time you think you will need to arrive on time at your new job. On-time means arriving at least 15 minutes earlier than your start time. The same rules apply if you are planning to take public transportation. Keep in mind, you will have to allow extra time to walk and/or drive to and from the public transportation stop.

2. Find out what is expected of you
Sit down with your supervisor and determine what your goals and objectives are for the first 30, 60, or 90 days. What are your department's goals and how will you help the department reach them? Ask for periodic meetings to receive feedback and to evaluate your progress based on your goals and objectives.

3. Create Your Own Growth and Development Plan
In addition to the "on the job training," how are you going to continue to grow professionally? Determine what technical and soft skills are valued in your new environment and develop a plan to sharpen those skills. This may mean reading books, researching on-line, or taking an additional course. You may have a similar job title from your old job but, no two jobs are alike. You want to bring fresh, new, and relevant ideas to your new department.

4. Look the part
Determine the most appropriate way to dress. Chances are, the first and second time you interviewed with the company, you were wearing your interview "uniform." Think back to how the

majority of the people were dressed. Was it traditional suit and tie, business casual, or completely informal? How were the interviewers dressed? It is best to dress in a more traditional business attire and adjust as you are able to observe your environment than to make a bad first impression.

5. Come prepared
Bring pen, notebook, and possibly your lunch. You may need to complete additional paperwork, write notes, or the names of the new people you meet. Unless it has been discussed prior to your start date, plan on bringing or buying your lunch.

6. Reserve your suggestions for improvement until a later time
You may have come from an environment that did things differently or you may clearly see areas to improve efficiency. Reserve your comments until you are able to find out the history or background of the subject. Time your suggestions so that you look like the "brilliant person" you really are.

7. Hang back before you hang out
There are office politics no matter where you work. It's not wise to allow yourself to be sucked into talking about a controversial topic or taking sides. Avoid commenting! Before you pick the group to hang out with for lunch and after work, listen and observe. You want to be associated with the right group of people instead of the mal-contents.

8. Act like you mean business
There is usually a lot of information given to you during your first weeks on your new job. No one expects you to have a photographic memory or remember everything. The best way to retain all the new information is to write it down. It shows that you take your job seriously and respect the time of the person who is training you. It also allows you to reference and review the information at any time. And don't be afraid to ask questions.

9. Thank those who have helped you
Write, call, or e-mail everyone who has helped you in your job search. You do this for several reasons:

1. You want to let everyone know that you have secured a job.
2. You want to thank them for any effort they have put forth on your behalf.
3. You want to favorably position yourself for the next time you might need to ask them for a favor.
4. You want them to know you are able to help them out in the future.

10. Be determined
The first few weeks are usually the hardest because you are learning so many new things and working with new people. You may also have a change in your old routine and your body must get use to that. Be focused, be determined, and be open to learning everything you can about your new job. You want to make a positive impression with your new boss, co-workers and also, a positive impact on your new job. Be open to your new experience.

RESOURCES

The people who get on in this world are the people who get up and look for the circumstances they want, and if they can't find them, make them.

George Bernard Shaw

Knowledge is <u>not</u> power. Knowledge is potential power. Power and success come from taking action on what you know.

Unknown

Resources

1. What Does a Career Coach Do? - Reasons to hire a Career Coach
2. Management/Leadership Books
3. Finding Work After 40 Books
4. Personal Development Books
5. Work/Life Balance Books
6. Research Company Websites
7. Cover Letter Books
8. Resume Books
9. 10 Books That Will Boost Your Job Search
10. Salary Websites: Find Out What You Are Really Worth

What Does a Career Coach Do?
Reasons to hire a Career Coach

Every successful athlete has a coach who helps him/her improve him/her technique, overcome fears, and push pass mental roadblocks. The coach helps the athlete to maximize his performance. A career coach is similar to a sports coach and can help you maximize your career success. Here are ten ways a career coach can help you.

1. Connects you to a deeper level of motivation than "just a job." You are able to build a career foundation when you discover your passion and purpose which will guide your decisions, and empower you to choose work you love, and make a good living.

2. Distinguishes himself from career counselors and consultants by building career management skills, which enables you to navigate future transitions.

3. Probes for deeper levels of motivation that, when addressed, can cause a lasting shift rather than providing just a quick fix.

4. Creates effective coaching interactions by listening, providing feedback, asking powerful questions, observing, and modeling.

5. Removes blocks to career progress, such as self-limiting beliefs, incomplete awareness of marketable skills, lack of purpose, and more.

6. Improves your ability to market and sell yourself in the job market regardless of economic conditions.

7. Increases your individual potential for career growth and future earning power by tailoring an approach consistent with your background and objectives.

8. Assists you in becoming "career self-reliant" by taking control and ownership of your career development.

9. Becomes your unwavering champion. A coach is always on your side and encouraging you to move forward toward your goals. When you falter or question your ability to reach your goals, your coach motivates you to keep going.

10. Works with you to ensure you have all the resources, information, and guidance you need to move in the right direction.

Management/Leadership Books

Leaders have the ability to influence, guide, and inspire others. Contrary to popular opinion, great leaders are made; they are not born. They have learned skills and demonstrated traits that make it easier for people to want to follow them. Each of us takes on leadership roles whether we are managers, workers, parents, or volunteers. Therefore, it is important that we learn how to lead more effectively. These management and leadership books have many practical tips and tools that will help you focus on your character traits and help you develop skills associated with good leadership.

1. **Leadership for Everyone:** *How to Apply the Seven Essential Skills to become a Great Motivator, Influencer, and Leader* by Peter Dean

2. **The New Leader's 100-Day Action Plan:** *How to Take Charge, Build Your Team, and Get Results* by George B. Bradt, Jayme A. Check and Jorge E. Pedraza

3. **Managing Right for the First Time** by David C. Baker

4. **The 5 Levels of Leadership:** *Proven Steps to Maximize Your Potential* by John C. Maxwell

5. **The New Manager's Toolkit:** *21 Things You Need to Know to Hit the Ground Running* by Don Grimme and Sheryl Grimme

6. **The 21 Irrefutable Laws of Leadership:** *Follow Them and People Will Follow You* by John C. Maxwell

7. **The First-Time Manager** by Loren B. Belker, Jim McCormick and Gary S. Topchik

8. **Executive Thinking:** *The Dream, the Vision, the Mission Achieved* by Leslie L. Kossoff

9. **The Art of War** by Sun Tzu

10. **The Extraordinary Leader:** *Turning Good Managers into Great Leaders* by John Zenger and Joseph Folkman

Finding Work After 40 Books

Finding employment can be challenging and it is particularly difficult for people over the age of 40. As an older worker, you have more experience, knowledge and have honed your professional skills. The key is to get focused, know what you want, have a clear plan and be flexible. You can increase your employability by following these ideas and strategies found in these books.

1. ***Over-40 Job Search Guide:*** *10 strategies for Making Your Age an Advantage in Your Career* by Gail Geary

2. ***Encore:*** *Finding Work that Matters in the Second Half of Life* by Marc Freedman

3. ***The Pathfinder:*** *How to Choose or Change Your Career for a Lifetime of Satisfaction and Success* by Nicholas Lore

4. ***Changing Course:*** *Navigating Life after 50* by William A Sandler, Ph.D. and James H. Krefft, Ph.D.

5. ***Over 40 & You're Hired:*** *Secrets to Landing a Great Job* by Robin Ryan

6. ***Finding Work After 40:*** *Proven Strategies for Managers and Professionals* by Robin McKay and Liam Mifsud

7. ***Great Jobs for Everyone 50+:*** *Finding Work That keeps You Happy and Healthy...And Pays the Bills* by Kerry Hannon

8. ***Finding a Job After 50:*** *Reinvent Yourself for 21st Century* by Jeannette Woodward

9. ***Escape the Mid-Career Doldrums:*** *What to do Next When You're Bored, Burned Out, Retired or Fired* by Marcia L. Worthing and Charles Buck

10. ***The Age Advantage:*** *Making the Most of Your Mid-Life Career Transition* by Jean Erickson Walker

Personal Development Books

What successes have you had? In what areas have you fallen short? What are your goals? How will you get there? I want to share with you my favorite personal development books. Each of these books makes me think, enables me to look at things differently and moves me forward each time I read them.

1. ***Awaken the Giant Within:*** *How to Take Immediate Control of Your Mental, Emotional, Physical & Financial Destiny* by Tony Robbins

2. ***Career Distinction:*** *Stand Out by Building Your Brand* by William Arruda and Kirsten Dixson

3. ***Feel the Fear…and Do It Anyway:*** *Dynamic techniques for turning fear, indecision, and anger into power, action and love* by Susan Jeffers, Ph.D.

4. ***Getting Things Done:*** *The Art of Stress Free Productivity* by David Allen

5. ***How to Win Friends and Influence People*** by Dale Carnegie

6. ***It's Only Too Late if You Don't Start Now***: *How to Create Your Second Life at Any Age* by Barbara Shea

7. ***Law of Attraction:*** *The Science of Attracting More of What You Want and Less of What You Don't* by Michael Losier

8. ***Power Networking:*** *59 Secrets for Personal and Professional Success* by Donna Fisher and Sandy Vilas

9. ***The 7 Habits of Highly Effective People***: *Powerful Lessons in Personal Change* by Steven Covey

10. ***The Success Principals:*** *How to Get From Where You Are to Where You Want to Be* by Jack Canfield

Work-Life Balance Books

Work-Life balance is a very personal and individual way for each of us to live our ideal life. There is no one size fits all solution. The following books will give you tips and strategies that will help you achieve your personal definition of work-life balance.

1. ***The Good Life Rules:*** *8 Keys to Being Your Best at Work and At Play*
   By Bryan Dodge and Matt Rudy

2. ***Life Matters:*** *Creating a Dynamic balance of Work, Family, Time, & Money*
   By A. Roger Merrill and Rebecca Merrill

3. ***Off Balance:*** *Getting Beyond Work-Life Balance Myth to Personal and Professional Satisfaction*
   By Matthew Kelly

4. ***The Work-at-Home Success Bible:*** *A Complete Guide for Women: Start Your Own Business; Balance Work, and Home Life; Develop Telecommuting Strategies*
   By Leslie Truex

5. ***The Work Revolution:*** *Freedom and Excellence for All*
   By Julie Clow

6. ***Get the Life You Love***
   By Arvind Devalia

7. ***HBR's 10 Must Reads On Managing Yourself***
   By Harvard Business Review

8. ***Choosing Work-Life Balance***
   By Walter H. Chan, Ph.D

9. ***Finding Right Work:*** *Five Steps to a Life You Love*
   By Leni Miller

10. ***Life! By Design:*** *6 Steps to an Extraordinary You*
    By Tom Ferry and Laura Morton

Research Websites

In an interview, you are expected to know something about the company. What kind of products and/or services does it provide, and how can your skills and knowledge help? The following websites can help you in your research about the company.

1. **All Business** – http://www.allbusiness.com

2. **Hoovers** - http://www.hoovers.com

3. **Corporate Information** - http://www.corporateinformation.com

4. **Forbes** - http://www.forbes.com/lists

5. **Highbeam Research** - http://www.highbeam.com/

6. **Annual Report Service** - http://www.annualreportservice.com

7. **Bloomberg** - http://www.bloomberg.com

8. **Thomas Register** - http://www.thomasnet.com

9. **Standard and Poor's** - http://www.standardandpoors.com

10. **Inc. Magazine** - http://www.inc.com/inc5000

Cover Letter Books

Every resume sent should have a cover letter whether it is mailed, e-mailed, or in response to a job post. A cover letter tells the reader why you are contacting them and gives you an opportunity to explain how you will contribute to the organization. Here are my recommendations for books that will help you compose a great cover letter.

1. *101 Best Cover Letters* by Jay Block and Michael Betrus

2. *Insiders Tips on Writing an Effective Cover Letter* by Tom Nixon

3. *15-Minute Cover Letter: Write an effective cover letter right now* by Michael Farr and Louise Kursmark

4. *Career Essentials: The Cover Letter* by Dale Mayer

5. *Cover Letters for Dummies* by Joyce Lain Kennedy

6. *Knock'em Dead Cover Letters: Cover letter samples and strategies you need to get the job you want* by Martin Yates, CPC

7. *Everything Cover Letter Book: Cover Letters for Everybody from Student to Executive* by Burton Jay Nadler

8. *No-Nonsense Cover Letters: The Essential Guide to Creating Attention-Grabbing Cover Letters That Get Interviews & Job Offers* by Wendy S. Enelow and Arnold G. Boldt

9. *Get It Done: Write a Cover Letter* by Jeremy Schifeling

10. *Killing the Cover Letter* by Gene Kincaid

Resume Books

Your resume is your marketing document that serves as an introduction to those who will hire you. Here are ten books that will help you craft a resume that will capture your unique skills, accomplishments, and work experience.

1. **Resume Magic:** *Trade Secrets of a Professional Resume Writer* by Susan Britton Whitcomb

2. **Federal Resume Guidebook:** *Strategies for Writing a Winning Federal Resume* by Kathryn Kraemer

3. **Knock'em Dead Resumes:** *How to Write a Killer Resume That Gets You Job Interviews* by Martin Yates

4. **How To Write A Resume:** *The Resume Writing Book That Helps You Crack Today's Tough Job Market* by Thomas Tucker

5. **Resumes For Dummies** by Laura DeCarlo

6. **Unbeatable Resumes:** *American's Top Recruiter Reveals What REALLY Gets You Hired* by Tony Beshara and Dr. Phil McGraw

7. **Expert Resume Series** by Wendy S. Enelow and Louise M. Kursmark

8. **How to Land a Top Paying Federal Job:** *Your Complete Guide to Opportunities, Internships, Resumes and Cover Letters, Application Essays (KSAs), Interviews, Salaries, Promotions and More* by Lily Whiteman

9. **Quick Resume & Cover Letter Book:** *Write and Use an Effective Resume in Just One Day* by Michael Farr and JIST Editors

10. **Resume 101:** *A Student and Recent-Grad Guide to Crafting Resumes and Cover Letters that Land Jobs* by Quentin J. Schultze and Richard N. Bolles

10 Books That Will Boost Your Job Search

Most people will stay on a job they hate rather than embark on a job search. I admit the idea of a job search is daunting; especially if you have not looked for a job in a while. I want to share with you some of the books that will make this process a little easier. Each of the books listed takes a different approach to your career search; so I am sure you will find one book which will inspire you to take action.

1. ***The Unwritten Rules of the Highly Effective Job Search*** by Orville Pierson

2. ***Job Search Strategies: Get a Good Job...Even In a Bad Economy*** by Bud Clarkson

3. ***The Hidden Job Market:*** *Proven Strategies, Done-For-You Letter and Phone Scripts* by Mary Elizabeth Bradford

4. ***Career Cowards Guide to Job Searching:*** *Sensible Strategies for Overcoming Job Search Fears* by Katy Piotrowski

5. ***30 Ideas****: The Ideas of Successful Job* by Tim Tyrell-Smith

6. ***Get the Job You Want, Even When No One's Hiring*** by Ford R. Myers

7. ***How to Get a Great Job in 90 Days or Less*** by Joe Carroll

8. ***Find a Job Through Social Networking:*** *Use LinkedIn, Twitter, Facebook, Blogs and More to Advance Your Career* by Diane Crompton and Ellen Sautter

9. ***Guerilla Marketing for Job Hunters 3.0:*** *How to Stand Out from the Crowd and Tap into the Hidden Job Market Using Social Media and 999 Other Tactics Today* by Jay Conrad Levinson

10. ***Weddle's Guide to Employment Sites on the Internet:*** *For Corporate and Third Party Recruiters, Job Seekers & Career Activists* by Peter Weddle

Salary Websites: Find What You are Really Worth

Am I getting paid enough? Am I asking too much, too little, or am I on target? How can you tell if the salary you have been offered pays enough or how your current salary compares to the market rate? You need to take the time to research salaries. This will enable you to make informed decisions concerning new job opportunities or validate the compensation you are currently receiving. These salary websites will take the mystery out of compensation data and help you get answers to your salary questions.

1. **CareerOneStop.org** – The Department of Labor site will provide you with median, high and low salaries as well as how your area compares with national numbers. Find this under the Salary + Benefits link.

2. **Glassdoor.com** – A member site that will search salaries by job function, company, or organization.

3. **Government Jobs** – Government pay is probably the easiest to determine because salaries are transparent. Jobs are listed along with a pay range. In fact, in some city and local government offices, the names and salaries of all public employees are posted on websites.

4. **Guidestar.com** – Shows salaries of the top five people in the non-profit organization.

5. **Indeed.com** – Under the salary tab, enter the job title, the city, and the average salary for the jobs that fit your criteria.

6. **Payscale.com** – An online salary, benefits, and compensation information company developed to help people obtain accurate real-time information on job market compensation.

7. **Salary.com** – Free general information by job title or geographic areas.

8. **Salaryexpert.com** – Provides reports on salaries and cost of living from compensation professionals.

9. **Salarysite.com-** an independent site that provides free information.

10. **Simplyhired.com** – An employment site for job listings. The company aggregates job listings from sites across the Web including job boards, newspapers and classified listings, associations, social networks, content sites, and company career sites.

About the Author

Karen Bragg-Matthews is a Life and Career Coach, speaker, facilitator, and President of KBM Career Concepts. With over 20 years of experience from managing small companies to being the head of several HR operations at a Fortune 500 company, Karen knows what companies look for in an employee. She has provided companies with the right people ranging from bus drivers to vice presidents, developed innovative training programs, and effectively trained thousands of people.

Karen holds a Bachelor's degree in Business Administration, is a Certified Training Manager, a Distinguished Toastmaster, and is a graduate of Coach University. She became a Career Coach to help more people find careers that make them feel happy, excited, and fulfilled. She brings true clarity and support to her clients. She has leveraged her keen knowledge of people to help them make real and lasting career choices and look at new possibilities.

As a Life and Career Coach, Karen helps her clients connect with a deeper level of motivation than "just a job." With Karen's guidance, clients discover their passion and purpose to guide their decisions, empower them to choose work they love, make a good living, and still have a balanced life. She helps her clients:
- improve their ability to market their skills and sell themselves in a job market regardless of economic conditions
- increase their potential for career growth and future earning power
- move toward their specific goals

Karen lives with her husband and two children in the Dallas, TX area. Karen has a passion for all things wine and knows best how to match wine with food. Her other company, Creative Wine Concepts LLC, conducts wine tastings and seminars. She earned her Sommelier Certification and is a graduate of the Sommelier Program at Algonquin College in Ottawa, Ontario, Canada.

Contact Karen at:
Email: kbm.coach@hotmail.com
Website: www.KbmCareerCoach.com
Join me on: Instagram.com/kbmcareers
LinkedIn.com/in/karenbraggmatthews